ON CUBA

ALSO BY NOAM CHOMSKY AND VIJAY PRASHAD

The Withdrawal

ALSO BY NOAM CHOMSKY

The Cold War and the University

Understanding Power

American Power and the New Mandarins

Towards a New Cold War

Problems of Knowledge and Freedom

Objectivity and Liberal Scholarship

For Reasons of State

The Chomsky-Foucault Debate

On Language

The Essential Chomsky

On Anarchism

The Responsibility of Intellectuals

ALSO BY VIJAY PRASHAD

The Karma of Brown Folk
Everybody Was Kung Fu Fighting
Uncle Swami
The Darker Nations
Red Star Over the Third World
Washington Bullets

ON CUBA

REFLECTIONS ON 70 YEARS OF
REVOLUTION AND STRUGGLE

NOAM CHOMSKY
AND VIJAY PRASHAD

THE
NEW
PRESS

NEW YORK
LONDON

Published in the United States by The New Press, New York, 2024
Distributed by Two Rivers Distribution

LIBRARY OF CONGRESS CATALOGING-IN-PUBLICATION DATA

Names: Chomsky, Noam, author. | Prashad, Vijay, author.
Title: On Cuba : reflections on 70 years of revolution and struggle / Noam
Chomsky, and Vijay Prashad.
Other titles: Reflections on 70 years of revolution and struggle
Description: New York : The New Press, [2024] | Includes bibliographical
references. | Summary: "A conversation between public intellectuals
examining the contentious interplay between the Cuban Revolution and
U.S. empire"-- Provided by publisher.
Identifiers: LCCN 2024007566 | ISBN 9781620978573 (hardcover) | ISBN
9781620978702 (ebook)
Subjects: LCSH: United States--Foreign relations--Cuba. | Cuba--Foreign
relations--United States. | United States--Foreign relations--1989- |
Cuba--Foreign relations--1959-1990. | Cuba--Foreign relations--1990- |
Cuba--History--Revolution, 1959--Influence.
Classification: LCC E183.8.C9 C4938 2024 | DDC
327.73/07291--dc23/eng/20240220
LC record available at https://lccn.loc.gov/2024007566

The New Press publishes books that promote and enrich public discussion and
understanding of the issues vital to our democracy and to a more equitable world. These
books are made possible by the enthusiasm of our readers; the support of a committed
group of donors, large and small; the collaboration of our many partners in the
independent media and the not-for-profit sector; booksellers, who often hand-sell New
Press books; librarians; and above all by our authors.

www.thenewpress.com

Book design by Bookbright Media
Composition by Bookbright Media
This book was set in Sabon and Oswald

Printed in the United States of America

2 4 6 8 10 9 7 5 3 1

ON CUBA

REFLECTIONS ON 70 YEARS OF
REVOLUTION AND STRUGGLE

NOAM CHOMSKY
AND VIJAY PRASHAD

THE
NEW
PRESS

NEW YORK
LONDON

Requests for permission to reproduce selections from this book should be made through
our website: https://thenewpress.com/contact.

Published in the United States by The New Press, New York, 2024
Distributed by Two Rivers Distribution

LIBRARY OF CONGRESS CATALOGING-IN-PUBLICATION DATA

Names: Chomsky, Noam, author. | Prashad, Vijay, author.
Title: On Cuba : reflections on 70 years of revolution and struggle / Noam
Chomsky, and Vijay Prashad.
Other titles: Reflections on 70 years of revolution and struggle
Description: New York : The New Press, [2024] | Includes bibliographical
references. | Summary: "A conversation between public intellectuals
examining the contentious interplay between the Cuban Revolution and
U.S. empire"-- Provided by publisher.
Identifiers: LCCN 2024007566 | ISBN 9781620978573 (hardcover) | ISBN
9781620978702 (ebook)
Subjects: LCSH: United States--Foreign relations--Cuba. | Cuba--Foreign
relations--United States. | United States--Foreign relations--1989- |
Cuba--Foreign relations--1959-1990. | Cuba--Foreign relations--1990- |
Cuba--History--Revolution, 1959--Influence.
Classification: LCC E183.8.C9 C4938 2024 | DDC
327.73/07291--dc23/eng/20240220
LC record available at https://lccn.loc.gov/2024007566

The New Press publishes books that promote and enrich public discussion and
understanding of the issues vital to our democracy and to a more equitable world. These
books are made possible by the enthusiasm of our readers; the support of a committed
group of donors, large and small; the collaboration of our many partners in the
independent media and the not-for-profit sector; booksellers, who often hand-sell New
Press books; librarians; and above all by our authors.

www.thenewpress.com

Book design by Bookbright Media
Composition by Bookbright Media
This book was set in Sabon and Oswald

Printed in the United States of America

2 4 6 8 10 9 7 5 3 1

Contents

Authors' Note

Our Essay on Cuba

On Cuba is not really about Cuba itself, but it is about the suffocation that the United States has tried to implement against Cuba. This suffocation is based on material interests, certainly, but centrally on the need by the U.S. government to destroy any defiance of its role in the world and on a culture of cruelty that has set in among high officials of the U.S. government against Cuba. The word "defiance" comes up repeatedly in U.S. policy documents and in statements by U.S. officials when they talk about Cuba, documents and statements that we quote extensively in this book. Anger at this defiance has built a culture of cruelty toward the Cuban Revolution, and consequentially toward the people who live in Cuba. This cruelty is illustrated by casual statements by these officials, such as when U.S. Secretary of State Alexander Haig told President Ronald Reagan in March 1981, "Just give me the word and I'll turn that fucking island into a parking lot." The records show that Reagan was "tempted."[1]

Despite the intensity of the U.S. campaign to overthrow the Cuban Revolution and despite the grave difficulties of building any kind of project in an island that has been embargoed by the most powerful country in the world since 1960, the Cuban people have resisted. We cannot think of another case like this in world history of a small country, practically engulfed by the world's most powerful state, which is trying to destroy it, yet managing to survive—and not only survive but succeed in many ways. The health statistics in Cuba are better than those in the United States, a fact discussed only in professional journals, if at all, and not among the general public. In his 2007 documentary *Sicko*, Michael Moore did dramatize the difference in health care between the United States and Cuba. Moore traveled to Cuba with 9/11 rescue workers. They go to Guantánamo and walk to the entrance of the U.S. detention camp, where the United States government held detainees from its Global War on Terror. Moore, through a megaphone, begs the officials at this camp—a massive human rights violation by itself—to allow the 9/11 rescue workers to get the same medical care as the detainees. It is great political theater. In Havana, the 9/11 rescue workers buy affordable medicines and medical treatment at the Hermanos Ameijeiras Hospital—which had been a bank in pre-Revolution Cuba—and then these workers are received at a Havana fire station, where they are treated as heroes. Rather than try to digest the implications of the film, the U.S. media (led by John Stossel of NBC News) went after Michael Moore and tried to prove that the section on Cuba in his film was misleading. Rather than investigate the implications of Moore's film, the U.S. media merely tried to debunk it.

The U.S. government's reaction to Moore's documentary was even more crude. On January 31, 2008, the United States Interest Section in Havana sent a cable to the U.S. State Department to say that the Cuban government had suppressed Moore's *Sicko* because they know "the film is a myth that does not want to risk a popular backlash by showing to Cubans facilities that are clearly not available to the vast majority of them." When this cable was released by WikiLeaks, Moore responded on his blog that this cable is a "stunning look at the Orwellian nature of how bureaucrats for the state spin their lies and try to recreate reality (I assume to placate their bosses and tell them what they want to hear)." Rather than suppress the film, Moore continued, "The entire nation of Cuba was shown the film on national television on April 28, 2008! The Cubans embraced the film so much so that it became one of those rare American movies that received a theatrical distribution in Cuba. I personally ensured that a 35 mm print got to the Film Institute in Havana. Screenings of *Sicko* were set up in towns all across the country."

---

*The health services in the United States are catastrophic. Even in major cities, but especially in the rural areas which are a total disaster, hospitals are collapsing. In many places, there are no medical services. If there was any minimal sanity, the United States would be inviting Cuban doctors to go to the rural areas in the United States.**

The U.S. public is taught over and over again by the government and by the mass media that Cuba is an authoritarian

---

* As mentioned below in the Authors' Note, all pull quotes in the book come from Noam's comments during our many hours of conversation.

state, that the people who live there are enslaved by communism, and that Cuba is a threat to the United States. None of these three propositions are true, and yet these falsehoods define the general U.S. public understanding of Cuba. Because of the overall framework against Cuba, the U.S. media cavalierly fabricates whatever they want in order to undermine Cuba in U.S. public opinion. For instance, in 2017, the U.S. government accused Cuba of a "sonic attack" on its diplomatic officials, a claim widely repeated verbatim in the U.S. press; six years later, a U.S. government intelligence review concluded that "foreign adversaries" are highly unlikely to have created the "Havana Syndrome," a point that the Cuban government made in 2017 but that was discounted and barely reported.[2] The stain of the original story remains. It sets the groundwork for the next ridiculous story, for instance about the construction of a Chinese military base in Cuba, which the Cuban government and the Chinese government denied immediately.[3] A reporter from BreakThrough News traveled to Bejucal, where the *Wall Street Journal* said there was a base, and asked people if they knew anything about this base or had seen any Chinese people in the town. The residents of this small town said that they had not seen any Chinese military activity in Bejucal, but—as one resident said—"on 22nd street there is a Chinese family, but they have lived here since I was a child." Another person said, yes, there are some people of Chinese descent in the town, one was a massage therapist in a gym: "they are Cuban Chinese," he said, born in Cuba, one of them eighty years old and the other a hundred years old.[4] None of these facts—least of all the voices of Cubans—are regarded in the midst of a dangerous frenzy. When a powerful country, with a grip over global information channels, crafts a lie, it stands; it is much more difficult to undo that lie, even when it is clear that the facts are ridiculous.

This book originates during an afternoon in Havana, when Vijay went to see the singer Silvio Rodríguez at his Estudios Ojalá to give him a copy of *La retirada*, the Spanish edition of our book *The Withdrawal*. It turns out that Silvio is an enormous fan of Noam, and so he gave Vijay a book about Cuban music that he had put together as a gift to Noam. This chance encounter led to a conversation between Noam and Vijay about Cuba, which morphed into a series of taped discussions that we adapted into a manuscript for this brief book.

Over the course of the first half of 2023, we had a series

of Zoom calls about U.S. foreign policy and Cuba. Despite Noam's busy schedule, these calls would drift over the course of several hours to touch on a range of subjects—from the Bay of Pigs attack to the placement of Cuba on the U.S. State Sponsors of Terrorism list—some of these conversations resulting in short articles and statements that we published during that time. Initially, we had planned to create a book based entirely on an edited version of this conversations: an interview book. Vijay prepared the lightly edited transcript, sent it to Noam, and in another conversation we realized that this book was not exactly what we wanted. We decided that the conversations had produced the conditions for us to write a different kind of book—a jointly written text, drawing from these conversations as well as our short articles and statements. A brief, jointly written book was the only way to honor our original vision. We went back and forth to discuss how to put the book together, using the transcripts of the conversations and unpublished texts that Noam sent Vijay. Vijay then used these materials to assemble a draft text, which both Noam and Vijay worked on until we had a suitable project to offer for publication. In each section of the book, you will find a short pull quote from Noam's comments during our many hours of conversation. We spent a month discussing this manuscript, trying to find a way to best approximate our combined assessment of the complexities of the Cuban Revolution. Despite our different points of departure, we found unity in our view that the U.S. government has been vindictive toward the Cuban Revolution because it has successfully defied Washington and it has offered a socialist model for the rest of the Third World. That is the core argument of this book. The text below is a more refined version of that draft, edited by Marc Favreau and Ishan Desai-Geller. We are grateful to Manolo De Los Santos, who had accompanied us on the journey to produce the book, for his introduction. And we are immensely happy that the president of Cuba, Miguel Díaz-Canel, wrote the foreword to *On Cuba*. Díaz-Canel took over from Raúl Castro, who himself took the top job in Cuba from the remarkable Fidel Castro. Those are difficult shoes to fill, and in particular to fill them when U.S. vindictiveness is at such a high level. But Díaz-Canel wears the shoes well, including using them to walk around the island to explain to people the nature of their crisis and to gather their hopes together to continue their struggle.

Foreword

I am deeply grateful to have been invited to write a few brief lines for this book on the long and painful history of U.S. aggression toward Cuba. It is an honor to introduce the work of Vijay Prashad and Noam Chomsky, writers of different generations who each ennoble the mission of the intellectual in our time through their marriage of political conviction and sober analysis.

My good friend Vijay Prashad and I have had the pleasure of sharing ideas and forums in recent times, and I am a great admirer of his theoretical work at Tricontinental: Institute for Social Research. I have, of course, known and admired Noam Chomsky for many years too. His impressive contributions to linguistic and communication theory and his timeless works of social criticism like *Manufacturing Consent* are mandatory in universities around the world and need little introduction. But what stands out in my mind is the political ardor he has inspired in his readers the world over.

At least twenty years ago, I remember reading of a lecture Chomsky delivered at the World Social Forum in Porto

Alegre, Brazil. I was astonished to discover that the lecture was held not in a classroom or conference hall, but in a soccer stadium which was completely overflowing with young people, attentive to his words and cheering him with the passion of fans. Or, put differently, with the passion that knowledge provokes.

In *On Cuba*, Chomsky and Prashad have joined forces to document and analyze U.S. imperial aggression against our heroic homeland. It is clear that they have approached this projecct with the spirit of respect and solidarity that has always defined their relationships with Cuba, and that they bring their trademark courage, honesty, and erudition to bear on the subject.

Indeed, we Cubans are forever grateful to Chomsky for some of the most comprehensive and accurate judgments on the U.S. blockade of Cuba. Several years ago, during an unforgettable visit to our country, he was asked to comment on the blockade. Strikingly, he was not satisfied with a simple condemnation. Instead, in just a few words he formulated an analysis that is as valid today as it was then. More recently, Chomsky and Prashad published an article picking up where Chomsky's analysis above ends to denounce in no uncertain terms the inclusion of our country on the United States' spurious State Sponsors of Terrorism list. In that valuable text, they remind U.S. President Joseph Biden that, despite more than sixty years of economic blockade, Cuba has been able to "overcome the indignities of hunger, ill-health, and illiteracy, the three social plagues that continue to trouble much of the world."

It is for precisely this reason that I am honored to place my name—as a son of the Cuban people, as a passionate follower of the first Socialist Revolution of the Western Hemisphere, and as a student of the ideas of José Martí and Fidel Castro— next to those of two authors, activists, and radical thinkers who are among the the world's foremost leftist intellectuals. Chomsky and Prashad have always defended our right to exist, develop, and prove that the struggles of humanity for its emancipation have not been in vain. A better world is possible. A Cuba free of blockade, harassment, and aggressions of all kinds could prove it.

—Miguel Mario Díaz-Canel Bermúdez
First Secretary of the Central Committee of the
Communist Party of Cuba and
President of the Republic of Cuba

Introduction

In 1959, the Cuban Revolution erupted onto the global stage, catching the world off guard. The island nation soon transformed into a hub for foreign journalists, eager students, and deep-thinking intellectuals, all determined to witness the unfolding social experiment with their own eyes. They were drawn to this Caribbean crucible of change like moths to a flame, all asking the question: what next?

The early 1960s saw a generation of intellectuals leaning toward the left, their gaze firmly set on Cuba's burgeoning revolution. Amid the tumultuous vortex of the Cold War, they attempted to decipher the political trajectory of this small nation shaking off the shackles of imperialism. Among U.S. intellectuals, many sought to shield the Revolution from the aggression of their own nation, insisting that the Cuban Revolution was not the spawn of communism as its critics alleged. Simultaneously, by the middle of 1960, certain foreign observers such as Leo Huberman and Paul Sweezy, editors of the *Monthly Review*, had begun labeling the Cuban

Revolution as "socialist," even before Fidel himself publicly declared the term.

One of the curious minds that made this journey was C. Wright Mills, the revered sociologist from Columbia University. Known for his seminal studies on the American class structure in the aftermath of World War II, his works *White Collar* and *The Power Elite* had already established him as an astute observer of societal shifts. For two weeks in August 1960, Mills immersed himself in the Cuban experience, even spending three days journeying with Fidel Castro himself. His mission was clear: to pen a book that would capture the voices of the Cuban revolutionaries and articulate their aspirations to the world. Unlike his peers, Mills perceived the Cuban revolutionaries through a different lens. He saw them as Marxists, engaged in the monumental task of constructing a "socialism with heart" on an island that had long been the victim of underdevelopment.

The triumph of the Cuban Revolution in 1959 was met with a belligerent stance from the U.S. government. Despite initially acknowledging the government of the newly inaugurated president Manuel Urrutia a mere week after the revolutionaries had dethroned the oppressive regime of Fulgencio

Batista, the U.S. proceeded to sabotage the Cuban Revolution, especially after Fidel Castro was elevated to the position of prime minister in February 1959. When Castro sought to visit the United States in April, President Dwight Eisenhower declined to meet him. This marked the beginning of a steady decline in relations, culminating in the United States severing ties with Cuba in 1961 and implementing a series of destabilizing tactics coordinated by the CIA: from over six hundred assassination attempts on Castro to terrorist activities under Operation Mongoose on the island and the Bay of Pigs invasion by right-wing Cuban exiles. With these insidious acts, the U.S. immediately set the tone for official policy toward the new, revolutionary Cuba. In 1962, the Kennedy administration initiated a blockade against Cuba, launching a relentless campaign of starvation and deprivation against the island's 11 million inhabitants that still chokes the island to this day.

However, it was not the people of the United States who condemned Cuba, despite the actions of their government. Just after the Revolution's victory, two potent sociopolitical forces within the United States—the Black liberation movement and socialist organizations—immediately rallied behind the Cuban Revolution.

When Castro journeyed to New York to participate in the 1960 UN General Assembly meeting before the U.S. had officially cut off ties with Cuba, he and his delegation were kicked out of their accommodations and left without a place to stay. Malcolm X stepped in and arranged for the Cuban delegation to lodge at Hotel Theresa in Harlem, a gesture that showcased the profound connections between the Black liberation movement and the Cuban revolutionaries across the sea. When Eisenhower denied Castro entry to his luncheon with other Latin American leaders, Castro responded by hosting his own gathering at a Harlem coffee shop for Hotel Theresa's employees, whom he referred to as "the poor and humble people of Harlem." In a meeting between Castro and Malcolm X, the latter affirmed, "there are 20 million of us and we always understand," highlighting the solidarity of the revolutionary process.

In March 1960, Leo Huberman and Paul Sweezy undertook a journey to Cuba to witness the Revolution firsthand. They interacted with key revolutionaries (Castro and Che Guevara), state officials, new civic bodies, and everyday Cubans. Upon their return to New York, Huberman and Sweezy published their observations in a special issue of their socialist publication, entitled "Cuba: Anatomy of a Revolution." Later that year, they released their report as a book with Monthly Review Press. This book was among the earliest to argue that the Cuban Revolution—fueled by its fierce commitment to sovereignty—was naturally evolving in a socialist direction. Huberman and Sweezy revisited the Revolution several times, with Huberman's *Socialism in Cuba* (1960) becoming highly regarded on the island for its empathetic critique of the Cuban process. The relationship between *Monthly Review* (the press and the magazine) and the Cuban Revolution has been enduring and significant.

Almost thirty years later, against the backdrop of the enduring blockade, the Third World debt crisis, and the dissolution of the Soviet Union, Cuba found itself compelled to embark upon a comprehensive reform agenda, albeit without ever wavering in its commitment to education, health, and collective well-being. The third congress of the Cuban Communist Party in 1986 adopted a new economic management and planning system, which incorporated wage reform, the integration of the market system into agriculture, the liberalization of production sectors, and the sale of public enterprises. These reforms carried an undertone of emergency given the decline in productivity in Cuba and the challenge of diversifying exports following a disappointing sugar harvest in 1970. The collapse of the USSR in 1991 forced Cuba into a "Special Period," which, despite popular belief that it ended in the 2000s, continues to persist. The worst of the Special Period was alleviated following the inception of the Bolivarian Revolution in Venezuela in 1999, though the hybrid war waged against Venezuela by the United States has hindered its ability to provide ample material support and solidarity to the Cuban population.

The disintegration of the Soviet Union also swiftly dispelled any hopes of a change in Washington, DC, as lawmakers enacted a series of harsh legislations aimed at tightening the stranglehold on Cuba. In fact, the United States' agenda of global hegemony has continually clashed with Cuba's pursuit of independence and sovereignty, and these clashes have only grown more intense since the Revolution's victory in 1959. The Cuban Democracy Act of 1992 (Torricelli Act) and the Cuban Liberty and Democratic Solidarity Act of 1996 (Helms-Burton Act) reinforced the framework of the U.S. blockade against Cuba. Even the occasional openings—mostly to benefit the U.S. agriculture lobby and select U.S. corporations on the prowl for markets—were quickly sealed whenever a bitter wind blew from Miami's Cuban exiles to the lawmakers on Capitol Hill. President Barack Obama attempted to restore a semblance of balance, initiating a dialogue about normalization with the Cuban government in 2009 and later visiting Cuba in 2016. The establishment of transportation networks and the operation of foreign businesses in Cuba represented small openings against the blockade.

But the United States has intensified its blockade against Cuba over the past six years, starting with former president Donald Trump. Upon assuming office, Trump promptly shuttered these openings and vowed to dismantle the Cuban Revolution, in addition to his promise to overthrow the Bolivarian Revolution in Venezuela and the Nicaraguan Revolution. The Trump administration labeled these the "troika of tyranny" and pledged their undoing through a campaign of "maximum pressure" led by the United States. In 2017, the U.S. accused the Cuban government of deploying sonic attacks against its embassy officials, a claim that was later disproven. However, this accusation served as a pretext to freeze relations with Cuba, causing a collapse in tourism and leading to significant loss of revenue as more than 600,000 annual U.S. visitors ceased their travels to the island. Trump also implemented 243 new sanctions, reversing the normalization process initiated by former president Obama in 2014. Under Trump's sanctions, Western Union halted operations in Cuba in 2020, disrupting remittances. Visa services were suspended by the U.S. embassy in Havana in 2017, sparking the largest wave of irregular migration since 1980.

In his last week in office in January 2021, former president Trump put Cuba on the U.S. State Sponsors of Terrorism list, making it nearly impossible for Cuba to engage in normal financial transactions necessary for trade. During President Joe Biden's first fourteen months in office, the Cuban economy lost an estimated $6.35 billion as a result, preventing Cuba from making crucial investments in its aging energy grid or purchasing food and medicine.

Despite campaign promises of a more balanced approach toward Cuba, President Biden has in fact amplified pressure on the nation. While avoiding Trump's rhetorical bluster, Biden masks the same policy behind the rhetoric of "human rights." But he is not fooling anyone.

Notwithstanding its endurance of the longest embargo in modern history, Cubans have managed to build world-renowned public education and health systems, as well as an innovative biotech industry, and have secured a higher quality of life for its citizens than many other developing countries. Still, Cuba's economy has suffered considerably under this far-reaching blockade. Due to the banking restrictions imposed by the blockade, the country's GDP shrank by a staggering 15 percent in 2019 and 11 percent in 2020, as the government and other entities found themselves unable to purchase basic necessities. When the COVID-19 pandemic hit in 2020, tourism, the country's number one industry, was eliminated. The pandemic also challenged Cuba's robust health care system, which was further pressured by the sanctions as Delta variant cases surged and the country's only oxygen plant was rendered nonoperational because of its inability to import spare parts. Even as Cuban patients struggled to breathe, Washington refused to make exceptions, offering U.S.-made vaccines only after most Cubans had already been vaccinated with domestically developed versions. Beyond the economic blockade, natural disasters such as Hurricane Ian in 2022 caused more than $1 billion in damages and left more than one hundred thousand families without homes.

With the economy shrinking, the government persevered

with its commitment to provide employment, but inflation rocked the Cuban peso, devaluing what were already considered low government wages. While the country's rationing system provided everyone with a subsistence diet, this was a level of deprivation that hadn't been felt by Cubans since the beginning of the Special Period in the 1990s, with no immediate solutions in sight. The Cuban government has since turned to alternative avenues for growth and development.

In 2020, Cuba began relying more heavily on the private sector to meet its basic needs due to the increasing scarcity of goods. With the private sector on track to import $1 billion of goods in 2023, and more than eight thousand small- and medium-sized businesses having registered since 2021, the economy is slowly growing at a rate of 1.8 percent. The rise of the private sector introduces new challenges for any socialist project.

Cuban president Miguel Díaz-Canel has expressed an evolving vision for Cuba's future, emphasizing the government's ongoing commitment to providing essential services to its citizens but also nodding toward changes. He argued that social justice is not merely about welfare or equality but also about a fair distribution of income, where those who earn more contribute more and those who are unable to contribute are assisted by the government.

In this journey, the Cuban government faces an uphill task. While the rise of the private sector has boosted supplies and provided badly needed goods, it in turn also creates new income disparities, which stands in contrast to revolutionary Cuba's historic emphasis on equitable wealth distribution. Moreover, if the government's new policies succeed in bringing back economic growth and more efficiently delivering needed supplies via the private sector—at a time when the state is essentially blocked from doing so—it will create a new social counterweight to the state itself. This changing dynamic will define Díaz-Canel's second and final term as president, as the government manages the balance between the private sector's growth and maintaining the socialist principles that are central to Cuba's identity.

So far, the leadership of the Cuban Revolution, while recognizing the necessity of wealth creation, has been committed to ensuring that the benefits of this wealth are shared among all its citizens. Díaz-Canel insists that the government will safeguard the socialist project—guaranteeing essential services, some free of charge and others at the lowest possible cost—while resisting the calls from friends and foes alike to embark on any major privatization efforts.

To this day, curious intellectuals, organizers, and artists still travel to the little Caribbean island to witness its ongoing revolutionary process. One such figure was Noam Chomsky, a steadfast critic of U.S. imperialism. Although his travels had taken him to the farthest corners of the world, the pulsating heart of Havana had eluded him until 2003, almost forty years into the U.S.-imposed blockade on Cuba. This long-awaited encounter was, in its own way, a testament to the enduring spirit of Cuba, a country that had survived against all odds, its spirit undimmed despite the onslaught of external pressures.

Vijay, my dear companion, and I have journeyed together around the world, and our stops on these journeys often transformed into extended listening sessions, where we absorbed the heart-wrenching tales of a world torn asunder by the overbearing might of U.S. imperialism, the omnipresent specter of war, and enforced underdevelopment—all symptoms of U.S. hegemony sadly evident in Cuba. We strolled along the dusty lanes of Playa Girón, accompanying a community doctor who bore the weight of memories both joyous and tragic. She could recall every child's birth she had presided over, their first cries echoing in her memories. Yet she also bore witness to the grim toll of a ruthless blockade, its scarcities claiming lives, leaving behind a trail of preventable sorrow. Beneath the dappled shade of mango trees, we sat with some of Cuba's Olympic boxers. Their eyes gleamed as they spoke of gold medals, the intricate dance of the jab, and the burning passion that fueled their victories. Their stories were interwoven with an undying love for their homeland and an unyielding resolve to triumph against all adversity.

At a scientific center, we stood in awe as experts unveiled their ambitious plans to vaccinate all the children of the Third World. Their vision was a testament to the Cuban spirit, a beacon of hope that rose above the crippling constraints of economic sanctions and political isolation. Among poets and intellectuals, we found ourselves engaged in fervent debates under the watchful eyes of John Lennon's statue. The discourse revolved around the pressing need to reposition Marxism at the heart of anticolonial discourse. The conversations were charged, the atmosphere electric with the potential for change.

Everywhere we went we listened, we observed, we learned.

We bore witness to the enduring resilience of the Cuban people, their courage and their indomitable spirit. We took note of their stories, their struggles, and their victories. Our journey was not just an exploration of a place but a deep dive into the heart of a people who, despite all odds, continue to dream, to resist, and to hope. In our many travels together, Vijay and I have gone down the worn paths of a bygone era, tracing the footsteps of the world revolution that once seemed within our collective grasp. Our wanderings were not born out of mere nostalgia but driven by the audacious hope of rekindling those flames. And Havana was no exception. In the end, we left not just with memories, but with a renewed sense of conviction in the resilience of humanity and an unwavering belief in the power of collective action.

While Western governments never lose an opportunity to criticize Cuba on both economic and political grounds, many in the Global South continue to support it as an example of resilience and independence. Faced with numerous challenges, Cuba has chosen a path of resistance, continually adapting and innovating in the face of adversity rather than succumbing to external pressures.

Amid the challenges of a global economy marked by crisis,

Cuba strives to maintain its socialist project, meet the needs of its people, and assert its independence. Despite facing the longest embargo in modern history, the nation has made significant strides in public education, health care, and sustainable development, outperforming many advanced economies. Despite the temporary setbacks, Cubans survive and live to fight the next battle.

—Manolo De Los Santos

On Cuba

Virtual Colony

The U.S. government has treated Cuba—which sits 90 miles off the coast of Florida—as its "virtual colony" almost since the founding of the United States in 1776. The term "virtual colony" should not be taken as hyperbole. It is a realistic assessment. It is a term that has been used by the conservative editors of *The Kennedy Tapes: Inside the White House during the Cuban Missile Crisis*, Ernest May and Philip Zelikow.[1] The second U.S. president, John Adams, looked south at Cuba and felt that it should be swallowed up by the newly formed nation. Adams's successor Thomas Jefferson was even more explicit. "If we seized Cuba," he wrote in 1817, "we will be the masters of the Caribbean."[2] Writing to the fifth U.S. president, James Monroe, Jefferson noted on October 24, 1823, "I candidly confess that I have ever looked upon Cuba as the most interesting addition that can be made to our system of States." If Cuba could not come by other means, such as through Jefferson's failed attempt to purchase Cuba from Spain in 1808 when he sent General James Wilkinson to Madrid, then it must be taken by war. The United States tried again to buy Cuba from Spain in 1848 (under President James Polk) and in 1854 (under President Franklin Pierce, an ancestor of President George W. Bush). Perhaps the clearest attitude toward Cuba in these early decades of the United States comes from John Quincy Adams, the sixth president, who wrote to the U.S. ambassador in Madrid as secretary of state in 1823, "But there are laws of political as well as of physical gravitation; and if an apple severed by the tempest from its native tree can not choose but fall to the ground, Cuba, forcibly disjoined from its own unnatural connection with Spain, and incapable of self-support, can gravitate only towards the North American Union, which by the same law of nature cannot cast her off from its bosom."[3] The Cubans call this theory *la fruta madura*, the ripe fruit.

Adams's predecessor James Monroe articulated the Monroe Doctrine in 1823, which claimed the American hemisphere for the United States. It was the fullest statement of Adams's own Manifest Destiny concept. These were religious-political judgments to justify the full-scale annexation—one way or the other—of the Americas, including of course Cuba. The desire for Cuba was not idiosyncratic. As Walter Johnson shows in his masterly book *River of Dark Dreams*, the business interests rooted in the Mississippi Valley's economic world looked down the river, past the Delta, into the Caribbean, focusing on Cuba and Nicaragua for expansion. Narciso López, the Venezuelan-Spanish general, worked with John O'Sullivan—who coined the term "manifest destiny"—to raid Cuba between 1849 and 1851; meanwhile, William Walker, inspired by the idea of "manifest destiny," raided Sonora (where he set up a republic) and Baja California, before setting his sights on Nicaragua, where he crowned himself president in 1856. Walter Johnson points out that this "filibuster" movement—the expansion of the United States—was driven by personal ambition, by the belief in "manifest destiny" and the idea of Anglo-Saxon superiority, but also by the anxiety of the planter class of the Mississippi Valley who worried about the decline of their power vis-à-vis the rising industrial classes of the northeast of the United States.[4]

19

NOAM CHOMSKY AND VIJAY PRASHAD

*The great grand strategist John Quincy Adams,
intellectual author of the Monroe Doctrine and of
Manifest Destiny, made the case that this annexation
by the United States of Cuba would be indispensable to
the continuance and integrity of the union itself.*

Through the course of the nineteenth century, the United
States pursued these objectives systematically, taking over
half of Mexico as part of its claim to the entire landmass.
By 1898, Cuba was about to liberate itself from the Spanish empire, but the United States intervened to prevent the
liberation of Cuba. In fact, the Cuban forces were not even
allowed to be at the surrender of the Spanish. Theodore Roosevelt resigned from his post as assistant secretary of the navy
and formed the First U.S. Volunteer Cavalry regiment—the
Rough Riders—which participated in the U.S. invasion of
Cuba. Roosevelt, who would later be president, intervened
as part of U.S. policy to prevent the independence of Cuba,
which had been dreamed about by José Martí, who died in
1895 at the hands of Spanish imperial forces at the Battle of
Dos Ríos.

In 1901, when Roosevelt was vice president of the United

States, the Congress passed the Platt Amendment, which allowed the United States to militarily intervene at any time if Cuba did not follow orders from Washington. Five years later, when Roosevelt was president, the Cuban government of Tomás Estrada Palma—a U.S. citizen—collapsed, so Roosevelt sent in U.S. forces to create a provisional government and opened up a period known as the Second Occupation of Cuba (1906–1909).[5] At that time, Roosevelt wrote of the island in language that is illustrative of his racist attitudes and of the U.S. government's general orientation toward Cuba: "I am so angry with that infernal little Cuban republic that I would like to wipe its people off the face of the earth. All we have wanted from them is that they would behave themselves and be prosperous and happy so that we would not have to interfere. And now, lo and behold, they have started an utterly unjustifiable and pointless revolution and may get things into such a snarl that we have no alternative save to intervene."[6] That phrase—*I would like to wipe its people off the face of the earth*—is chilling.

The Roosevelt Corollary (1904) to the Monroe Doctrine (1823) is not often remembered, but it is necessary to recount it for our argument. The text of the corollary is from

Roosevelt's December 6, 1904, address to Congress. The relevant section is worth quoting in full:

All that this country desires is to see the neighboring countries stable, orderly, and prosperous. Any country whose people conduct themselves well can count upon our hearty friendship. If a nation shows that it knows how to act with reasonable efficiency and decency in social and political matters, if it keeps order and pays its obligations, it need fear no interference from the United States. Chronic wrongdoing, or an impotence which results in a general loosening of the ties of civilized society, may in America, as elsewhere, ultimately require intervention by some civilized nation, and in the Western Hemisphere the adherence of the United States to the Monroe Doctrine may force the United States, however reluctantly, in flagrant cases of such wrongdoing or impotence, to the exercise of an international police power.[7]

Countries that abide by U.S expectations can rest assured that they will not be harmed. If, however, a country in the Americas does not "keep order" or "pay its obligations," then the United States has permission and an obligation to intervene

22

militarily. These were not idle words. If you just look at the ten years after the Roosevelt Corollary went into effect, you see the United States intervening militarily in Cuba (1906–1909), Nicaragua (1907), Honduras (1907), Panama (1908), Nicaragua (1910), Honduras (1911), Cuba (1912), Panama (1912), Honduras (1912), Nicaragua (1912–1933), Mexico (1913), Dominican Republic (1914), Mexico (1914–1918), and Haiti (1914–1934). The first major achievement of the Roosevelt Corollary to the Monroe Doctrine was the U.S. intervention into Venezuela in 1920, when President Woodrow Wilson kicked out the British, at that time weakened by World War I.[8] That war accelerated the shift in the world from coal to oil as a major source of energy. North America, mainly the United States, was by far the major producer of oil, but Venezuela was an important reservoir of oil (it also had other key resources such as iron and gold). Since the United States tossed out the British, it was U.S. corporations that enriched themselves in Venezuela for decades, supporting dictators (such as Marcos Pérez Jiménez, 1952–1958) and capitalist elites (of the two main parties, COPEI and Acción Democrática), until the election of Hugo Chávez in 1998 that turned the balance of forces against U.S. imperialism in the country.

The centrality of Venezuela to this entire worldview of
Washington was illustrated in the conversations inside the
White House during the Cuban Missile Crisis. The Kennedy
brothers—John and Robert—worried about the Soviet missiles in Cuba, not only because they might (although very
unlikely) be used against the United States. They were openly
worried that the Soviet missiles in Cuba might deter a U.S.
invasion of Venezuela, if such an action became necessary
along the grains of Roosevelt's Corollary—to "keep order"
and to ensure that Venezuela's pliant leadership "pay its obligations" to its international creditors. The anxiety in the
Oval Office and in the CIA grew after the defeat of the mercenary force that was sent to the Bay of Pigs in April 1961. At
a key meeting of the high officials of the U.S. government in
the White House on October 16, 1962, they discussed how to
respond to intelligence about the presence of Soviet missiles
in Cuba. If the United States preemptively bombed the sites in
Cuba, Attorney General Robert Kennedy said, "You're going
to kill an awful lot of people, and we're going to take an
awful lot of heat on it." And, Kennedy said, the Soviets might
respond in the same way in Turkey and Iran, where the Unit-

ed States had missiles pointed toward the USSR.[9] The anxiety in the Oval Office was not about the larger questions—a missile fired from Cuba at Florida—but at the greater questions: would these missiles prevent the United States from being able to exercise the Monroe Doctrine and the Roosevelt Corollary against Venezuela, and other countries in the region, if it tried to exert its sovereignty? Robert Kennedy assumed that Fidel Castro might say to the United States, "If you move troops down into that part of Venezuela we're going to fire those missiles." President John F. Kennedy drew the clear conclusion: "It makes them look like they're co-equal with us."[10] The appearance of equality ("co-equals") was unimaginable to the high officials of the United States. Manifest Destiny and the Monroe Doctrine meant that the Cubans had to be kept in their place.

After 1898, Cuba became the "virtual colony" that the U.S. presidents had imagined. Its entire infrastructure was controlled by U.S. multinationals, which charged enormous fees for the provision of electricity and water and paid basement prices for the old plantation crop, sugar. Total suffocation of Cuban political life meant that the country became a tourist base, a destination for U.S. citizens to do there what was perhaps frowned upon inside the puritanical United States. As a tourist base, Cuba attracted the worst of the mafia, which set up shop there and made Cuba into a gangsters' paradise.[11] Any attempt by the Cuban people to reform the system and to exercise the most modest sovereignty was faced with repression, which escalated into the establishment of the dictatorship of Fulgencio Batista. While U.S. government documents hold evidence of dismay in Washington among the white-shoe elites about the "excesses" of the Batista regime, there was no appetite to allow any real change to take place either on the island or in the island's relationship with the United States.[12] That attitude of disdain for Cuba and the ambitions of the Cuban people was on display inside the White House during the missile crisis. Marine Corps Commandant David Shoup, who opposed many of the adventures of the United States during that period, nonetheless called Cuba a "little pipsqueak of a place."[13] Right till the day when the Cuban revolutionaries moved closer and closer to Havana, the U.S. government supported Batista and his army, despite the pretense of an arms embargo in March 1958.[14]

The Mafia Principle

Cuba today is a country of 11 million people. It has a smaller population than greater New York City. And yet, for over a century, the United States has treated Cuba as a threat to be contained—whether from its independence movement in 1898 or from the revolutionary movement in 1959. Countries in the Caribbean have faced U.S. intervention through the Roosevelt Corollary of the Monroe Doctrine not because of their size or any tangible military threat that they pose to the United States, but for the simple fact that they defied the United States. For instance, the United States invaded Grenada in October 1983 to overthrow the New Jewel movement, a socialist political movement led by Maurice Bishop. Grenada had a population at that time of around 90,000, far smaller than midsized cities in the United States (it had a population the size of Kenosha, Wisconsin). The New Jewel movement had no army to threaten anyone, nor was it poised to become a military base for anyone. What explains these interventions and the attitude toward Cuba is that these countries—particularly Cuba—*defied* the United States. If you read the U.S. State Department documents after 1959, it is clear that the U.S. government is apoplectic about Fidel

Castro's "successful defiance" of U.S. policy. A Special National Intelligence Estimate to the U.S. president from March 1960 clearly made this point:

> The Communists probably also believe that the U.S. will lose in influence and prestige so long as Castro's successful defiance of the U.S. (including his acceptance of bloc assistance) continues, and that the U.S. is faced with the dilemma of tolerating an increasingly Communist-oriented Cuba or of arousing widespread Latin American opposition by intervening.[15]

The general view is that if Cuba succeeds in defying U.S. power, then it might instigate others in the region to develop a similar agenda against the U.S. neocolonial order, and the whole system of domination will erode.

The attitude of the United States to any national project that tried to assert its sovereignty was clear at the Inter-American Conference on War and Peace held in Mexico in February–March 1945, which produced the Act of Chapultepec. Mexico's foreign minister Ezequiel Padilla told the conference that it was "vital for the Americans to do more than produce raw materials and live in a state of semi-colonialism."[16]

When he spoke of "Americans," he meant the people of the hemisphere and not just of the United States. The view was that the peoples of the hemisphere must be allowed to use all tools necessary—including tariffs and subsidies—to build industries in the region. Undersecretary of State for the United States Dean Acheson was horrified by this attitude, telling the Venezuelan delegation that it had been "short-sighted" by "increasing tariffs and restricting trade by import and other controls after the first World War and in the early thirties." The United States put forward a resolution to get all the Latin American states "to work for the elimination of economic nationalism in all its forms," including the exercise of economic sovereignty against the advantages secured by multinational corporations. The first beneficiaries of a country's resources, the U.S. political class argued, should be U.S. investors. So the economic order forced down the throat of Latin American leaders in 1945 was that a country's resources were not for that country but for the multinationals. Countries can produce goods, but not in competition with the United States, and countries could not create barriers to prevent the intervention of U.S. corporations or U.S. products. The only free market to be allowed was the free market for U.S. corporations.[17]

Countries can produce goods, but not in competition with the United States. So, for example, they concluded that Brazil can have a steel industry, but only to produce low-level steel that does not compete with the more sophisticated and advanced U.S. steel industry. None of this new nationalism business. With one exception, of course. The United States, which was permitted to do anything to ensure its economic supremacy.

The worry about contagion of defiance—including merely by trying to establish economic sovereignty—comes out clearly and punctually at moments when the elites in the U.S. establishment feel that their imperial interests are being imperiled. For instance, when Cuba intervened—correctly, in our opinion—to assist the national liberation forces in Angola and in the rest of southern Africa, U.S. Secretary of State Henry Kissinger clearly displayed the murderous intent of that elite. On March 15, 1976, Kissinger met with President Gerald Ford and told him that the Cuban operations overseas worried many U.S. allies. To be precise, these "U.S. allies" included the white-settler regimes (such as Rhodesia and

South Africa). "I think we have to humiliate them," Kissinger said. "If they move into Namibia or Rhodesia," both white-settler colonies with apartheid-type systems, "I would be in favor of clobbering them. That would create a furor and we might have to come out for black rule."[18] A few days later, on March 24, Kissinger met with the high officials of Ford's national security and military team, where he anticipated the need for "an invasion or blockade" of Cuba. "If we decide to use military power, it must succeed. There should be no halfway measures—we would get no award for using military power in moderation. If we decide on a blockade, it must be ruthless and rapid and efficient." These are chilling words, but they are words that are used regularly regarding Cuba. The general conclusion of these men is the following: if the Cuban Revolution cannot be defeated, then Cuba itself should be annihilated. This has been the formula for U.S. foreign policy toward Cuba since 1959.

In general, U.S. foreign policy is dictated by the main sectors of the corporate world, which pretty much owns the government.[19] But there are a few cases of conflict between the narrow corporate interests and the wider governmental—in this case imperial—interests. Corporate interests are parochial,

31

based on the petty needs of corporations to control the flow of raw materials and cheap credit for themselves, to keep labor costs low, and to widen market access. There are many instances where the particular interests of one corporation or one sector is identical to the broader imperial interests, such as when the United States government decided to overthrow the government of Guatemala in 1954 after President Jacob Arbenz threatened the dominion of United Fruit Company (it helped that several senior members of the Eisenhower administration were direct beneficiaries of United Fruit, including the Dulles brothers with John Foster having done legal work for the firm and Allen being on the board, both on the payroll of the company for thirty-eight years).[20] With Cuba, in the early years, the corporations were furious about the moves made by the revolutionaries to exercise sovereignty over their own country. These corporations had extensive interests in Cuba, with the total book value of the U.S. companies in Cuba being greater than in any other Latin American country at that time.[21] The corporations knew what was coming, since Castro had been very explicit in his description of what a revolutionary law would resemble in *History Will Absolve Me* (1953): for instance, the third law proposed that a third of the profits of all industrial, mercantile, and mining firms would go to workers and employees. In 1957, U.S. businessmen told Ruby Hart Phillips that "they couldn't understand why anyone would support a revolution. They wanted Batista to crush the Fidel Castro rebellion so that they could 'get on with business.'"[22]

What you have to recognize is that international affairs are run pretty much like the mafia. Very much the same logic as in The Godfather. *The Godfather, the mafia boss, is not necessarily a sadist. But if anybody doesn't pay the protection money, then you have to smash them up, otherwise things will get out of hand. If a small shopkeeper does not pay up, well then, somebody else might not pay up. So you have to stop it right from the beginning. It's a very sensible policy. All imperialist states, from the Dutch to the English to the United States, have run that way.*

Right into the present, a large number of firms continue to fight for restitution of their lost assets, and these firms lobby for the kind of strangulation that the United States

33

conducted against Cuba. The demand for compensation was redoubled after the U.S. Congress passed the Helms-Burton Act (1996). Title III of that act allows the owners of properties confiscated by the Cuban Revolution to sue companies "trafficking" or profiting from them for three times their current value (in 2019, for instance, the Carnival Cruise Line was sued for using confiscated property). The firms that hastened to get in line for reparations—all U.S. concerns, even if some sound like Cuban companies—include the Cuban Electric Company (owned by Office Depot), North American Sugar Industries, MOA Bay Mining Company, United Fruit Sugar Company, West Indies Sugar Corporation, American Sugar Company, Exxon Corporation, the Francisco Sugar Company, Starwood Hotels & Resorts, Texaco, Coca-Cola, Colgate-Palmolive, and the International Telephone and Telegraph Company. Their claims against the Cuban Revolution frame much of the legislation in the United States that collectively forms the U.S. policy of a blockade on Cuba.

Eventually, as the decades went by, and as it became clear that the Cuban Revolution was not going to be overthrown easily, several U.S. corporations began to show signs of eagerness to do business with Cuba. For instance, in 2016,

Arkansas governor Asa Hutchinson, speaking for the rice lobby in his state, said that Cuba was the world's largest per capita consumer of rice and his state's rice producers—such as Riceland Foods—were eager to enter the Cuban market.[23] Furthermore, the multinational pharmaceutical corporations would have liked to market the hundreds of drugs that the Cuban pharmaceutical industry had developed, including lifesaving drugs unavailable in countries such as the United States. When President Barack Obama opened the door to increased trade in 2017, these companies lined up eagerly to sign deals and get access. But these very powerful corporations—with their pecuniary interests—have not been able to overcome the broader imperialist policy of the United States government, which acts to ensure that Cuba's defiance is smothered. Even the short-term gains to parts of the capitalist class must be sacrificed for the long-term gain of extinguishing any and every rebellion. Despite the desire of these sectors of the U.S. capitalist class—for reasons of profit and market maximization—to trade with Cuba, they are blocked by the U.S. government.

International affairs are generally run like the mafia runs a protection racket. If you don't pay protection money (or "keep order" and "pay your obligations"), then you are going to get smashed up. The problem with Cuba for the United States was not whether or not the Revolution had adopted a communist orientation, although that certainly helped build the negative fantasy about the island's political project. The real problem with Cuba for the United States elites was its defiance of the U.S. mandate and its attempt to assert its national sovereignty over its resources in order to build up the dignity of its people. Five years before the Cuban Revolution, the U.S. government—with the Central Intelligence Agency as the spear—overthrew the government of President Jacob Arbenz of Guatemala because his government wanted to democratize land rights. It was unthinkable for the U.S. multinational firm United Fruit Company that its vast, and often unused, plantations would be taken over by the government to satisfy the democratic aspirations of landless farmers. As Secretary of State John Foster Dulles said in 1954 after the coup in Guatemala, what the United States was most concerned about was the prospect that anyone might try to stand up against the U.S. empire. The fantasy of Soviet intervention fulfilled ideological objectives, but the real problem was that of defiance. "This intrusion of Soviet despotism," Dulles said along the grain of the fantasy, "was, of course, a direct challenge to our Monroe Doctrine, the first and most fundamental of our foreign policies."[24] The absence of defiance and the complete authority of the United States was the alpha and omega of its foreign policy.

What the Cuban Revolution Did

In 1956, Fidel Castro and eighty-one other revolutionaries landed in Cuba's easternmost province of Oriente in their boat *Granma*. Only twenty-one of them survived the landing, which had been quickly spotted by Batista's forces and attacked. The survivors hastened into the hills of the Sierra Maestra to set up a base area in coordination with the mass struggles that they hoped would eventually break out in the rest of Cuba. Twenty-four months and thirty days later, the forces of Batista dissolved, and the Cuban Revolution was victorious. In February 1957, ten weeks after the *Granma* landed and long before the Revolution succeeded, Fidel Castro met the *New York Times*'s Herbert Matthews in the Sierra Maestra. Over three hours, Matthews talked to Castro about a range of issues, including the 26th of July Movement's views on nationalism, anticolonialism, and anti-imperialism.* Castro told him, "You can be sure we have no animosity toward the United States and the American people. Above all, we are fighting for a democratic Cuba and end to the dictatorship." There was no mention of communism, although Matthews wrote that the 26th of July Movement is "a revolutionary movement that calls itself socialistic. It is also nationalistic, which generally in Latin America means anti-Yankee."[25]

It did not matter that in the same article Matthews suggested that the revolutionaries were "anti-Communist." Castro knew that the United States would go after him merely for trying to establish the sovereignty of Cuba, let alone for his agenda—laid out in 1953 in *History Will Absolve Me*—of building the dignity of the Cuban people. Nothing that Castro put on the table in that speech was outside the bounds of the Cuban Constitution of 1940 (which remained in place till 1976, seventeen years after the Revolution). In that 1953 speech, Castro, the lawyer, elaborated on the laws already in place but disregarded by the Batista dictator-

---

* The 26th of July Movement was named for the 1953 failed attack at the Moncada barracks, led by Fidel Castro; it was formed as a vanguard organization to lead a revolutionary process in Cuba.

ship (1952–1959), nor by Batista's two predecessors Carlos Prío Socarrás (1948–1952) and Ramon Grau San Martín (1944–1948). Fidel was perfectly clear in the speech he made to the court after his failed attempt at taking power in 1953:

All these laws and others would be based on the exact compliance of two essential articles of our Constitution: one of them orders the outlawing of large estates, indicating the maximum area of land any one person or entity may own for each type of agricultural enterprise, by adopting measures which would tend to revert the land to the Cubans. The other categorically orders the State to use all means at its disposal to provide employment to all those who lack it and to ensure a decent livelihood to each manual or intellectual laborer. None of these laws can be called unconstitutional. The first popularly elected government would have to respect them, not only because of moral obligations to the nation, but because when people achieve something they have yearned for throughout generations, no force in the world is capable of taking it away again.

The problem of the land, the problem of industrialization, the problem of housing, the problem of unemployment, the problem of education, and the problem of the people's health: these are the six problems we would take immediate steps to solve, along with restoration of civil liberties and political democracy.[26]

In the first months of the Revolution, this is precisely what the new government did—tackle the problems of land, housing, education, health, industrialization, and unemployment.[27] But to fully deal with these, the government had to expel U.S. corporations that had bled the country and refused to abide by the principles of the 1940 Constitution and the 1945 UN Charter. And these moves provoked a reaction from the United States, a reaction that Che Guevara had seen in 1954 as an eyewitness in Guatemala when the United States overthrew the liberal government of Jacob Arbenz when he merely tried to democratize land ownership through Decree 900 (which passed the Guatemalan Congress and was based on Guatemala's 1940 Constitution).[28] Even Arbenz's agrarian reform, which placed a land ceiling of 224 acres, was seen to be too much both for the corporations and for the government of the United States. So anything that the Cuban Revolution did to rattle the cage of the U.S. corporations was

40

going to bring the wrath of people including Allen Dulles, the longest-serving CIA director who was in office from 1953 to 1961 and who oversaw the coups in Iran (1953) and Guatemala (1954), as well as failed attempts in Syria (1956–1957) and Indonesia (1957–1959). At a meeting on December 31, 1958, hours before the Cuban Revolution succeeded, Allen Dulles met with high officials of the U.S. government, and they all agreed—as Hugh Thomas recounts—that "Castro was not the right man for Cuba."[29] In fact, "Castro" was shorthand for the kinds of policies that he would enact as part of the new revolutionary government. It was not acceptable to the United States elites for the Cuban people to build a society of their dreams, which was precisely the agenda of Castro and the movement that he led.[30]

Castro's shadow loomed large because the social and economic conditions throughout Latin America invited opposition to ruling authority and to encourage agitation for radical change. When Kennedy came to office, he established a special mission to work out policy for Latin America led by Arthur Schlesinger, who warned of the susceptibility of Latin Americans

*to Castro's idea of taking matters into one's own
hands. The danger of the Castro idea grew because
of the distribution in Cuba of land and other forms
of national wealth from the propertied classes to the
poor and the underprivileged. Others in Latin America
began to demand opportunities for a decent living.
That's the problem for the United States in Latin
America, new inspiration by the Castro model.*

———————————

Castro knew that the CIA would not be able to do in Cuba
what it had done in Guatemala in 1954. In October 1959,
Castro met with Soviet intelligence agent Aleksandr Alekseyev. Alekseyev, a veteran KGB agent, reported to Moscow
that Castro presciently told him, "All U.S. attempts to intervene are condemned to failure." Why was Castro so certain
of his position? The Cubans knew that over 90 percent of the
population had supported the Revolution against the dicta-
tor Batista. The encrusted elite had fled rapidly to the United
States, ninety miles away, where they set up shop in Miami's
new Little Havana. In April 1960, the U.S. State Department
drafted a memorandum on Cuba. It found that "the majority of Cubans support Castro" and that "there is no effective

political opposition" on the island. Communist influence, the memorandum noted, was "pervading the Government and the body politic at an amazingly fast rate." What could the United States do to undermine the Castro government on behalf of the old Cuban elites and the U.S.-based corporations? "The only foreseeable means of alienating internal support," wrote the State Department's Lester D. Mallory, "is through disenchantment and disaffection based on economic dissatisfaction and hardship." The U.S. government must, therefore, use "every possible means" to "weaken the economic life of Cuba." Castro knew this. During his meeting with the KGB's Alekseyev, Castro said that he did worry about Cuba's economy. As with many colonies, Cuba had been forced into a one-crop economy—in its case, sugar. The Batista government had relied upon sales of sugar to the United States and on tourism from the United States. Both would have to end if Cuba was to succeed. "The only danger for the Cuban Revolution," Castro told Alekseyev, "is Cuba's economic weakness and its economic dependence on the U.S., which could use sanctions against Cuba. In one or two years, the U.S. could destroy the Cuban economy."

All the usual data—literacy rate, infant mortality rate,

nutrition intake—show that in the early years of the Revolution improvements came fast and furiously. Remarkably, over the course of 1961, Cuba's enthusiastic young revolutionaries eradicated illiteracy from the island, even from rural Cuba where the rates of illiteracy had been shockingly high. The census of 1946 and data from 1953 and 1957 show that a large section of the Cuban population relied on the land, with agriculture being the largest employer.[31] A study by professors in Havana from 1957 noted, "The city of Havana is living an epoch of extraordinary prosperity, while in the countryside, people, especially the agricultural workers, are living in sluggish, miserable, and desperate conditions too difficult to believe."[32] That is why the new revolution's agrarian reform law was so eagerly anticipated. In May 1959, the Agrarian Reform Law—drafted by Che Guevara—passed, which restricted land holdings to 3,333 acres, a ceiling that expropriated 40 percent of the land held by foreign corporations (such as the U.S.-owned sugar barons). Castro's government offered compensation, but this was offered not in cash but in twenty-year reimbursable treasury bills. Washington was furious, the Godfather angered at this very smart move by Castro. The U.S. oil companies that still owned the refineries in Cuba refused to refine Soviet oil that entered the country, and the sugar companies cut their purchases of Cuban sugar. U.S. Ambassador Philip Bonsal wrote a long note to Washington on August 2, 1960, saying, "I am as convinced as anyone could be that we cannot do business with Castro and the people who currently control him."[33] Four days later, the Cuban government enacted Law 980 that nationalized all U.S. businesses in the country. By December 1960, the United States ceased import of Cuban sugar, and diplomatic relations ended on January 3, 1961. On December 5, 1960, a month before he had to leave Havana, Ambassador Bonsal defined the elements of U.S. policy—along with "its Latin American and NATO allies" toward Cuba in a few sentences:

(a) tightening of economic sanctions; (b) massive increase of democratic propaganda; (c) strengthening and encouragement of the Cuban opposition; (d) termination of diplomatic relations with Cuba; and finally, if necessary, to achieve the objective, (e) interdiction of Sino-Soviet assistance.[34]

On April 17, 1963, Fidel Castro told the American Society of Newspaper Editors, "I have said very clearly that we are not Communists." "Our revolution," he said, "is a humanistic one."[35] Two days later, Kennedy told the same group, "I don't accept the view that Mr. Castro is going to be in power in five years." Kennedy was assassinated seven months later. Castro stepped down from the presidency in 2008, forty-five years later.

Covert Action

The most striking fact about the U.S. policy toward Cuba has been the astonishing frenzy and hysteria. It is the emotional content that is quite remarkable, starting right from the beginning, even before the Batista dictatorship had been overthrown. By May 1959 the CIA had begun to arm counterrevolutionaries within Cuba and to assemble the Cuban exiles in Florida into a political and military bloc. The U.S. government—often through the CIA—egged on the Cuban exiles to attack Cuban institutions outside the country (embassies in Haiti and the Dominican Republic were attacked as early as June 7, 1959) and to conduct attacks on Cuban soil (with aerial bombing of Havana on October 21, 1959, and bombing with napalm on sugarcane fields on January 12, 1960). These incendiary attacks were all CIA initiated and supervised. The aircraft were piloted by exiled Cubans from Florida. The Miami CIA operations center—JMWAVE—ran these terrorist attacks as well as began to shape the armed force that would try to invade Cuba in April 1961 at the Bay of Pigs. Cuba's first intelligence chief—Fabian Escalante—documented that the CIA tried to assassinate Fidel Castro at least 634 times.[36]

In March 1960, the Eisenhower administration authorized the CIA to overthrow the government in Cuba. The CIA document said that goal was the "replacement of the Castro regime with one more devoted to the true interests of the Cuban people and more acceptable to the U.S."[37] It is unlikely that there was any interest in the Cuban people, who had come out in historic numbers on January 8, 1959, to greet Castro as he rode into Havana with the Freedom Caravan. This goal to create a government with "the true interests of the Cuban people" was invalidated by the CIA's own task of creating—out of nothing—an "appealing" Cuban opposition, and of course by the CIA's terror campaign that impacted the lives of the Cuban people. Keith Bolender, a Canadian journalist, published a book in 2010 that collects

47

the testimonies of Cubans who survived the U.S. terror campaign that took the lives of at least three thousand Cubans.[38]

The U.S. government sponsored terrorism. Robert Kennedy warned that if there was a full-scale invasion of Cuba, it would kill an awful lot of people. A member of the National Security Council staff suggested that if there were raids on Cuba that were haphazard and killed innocents, it might mean bad press in some friendly countries. That's the one moral objection that was raised in the U.S. establishment. The problem with killing an awful lot of people when you invade a country is that you take a lot of heat for it. That's the problem. Not the killing itself. In 1971, President Nixon's administration introduced an African swine fever virus, causing an outbreak of disease, whose impact would have been worse for Cuba had not the nutrition levels improved over the previous twelve years and had not the Cuban health care system been significantly transformed.

The two most famous Cuban exile terrorists in the pay and

control of the CIA were Luís Posada Carriles and Orlando
Bosch.[39] Carriles had been in Batista's police service and
worked for the CIA from 1960 to 1963, while Bosch was
a thug who intimidated with violence anyone who spoke
against the overthrow of the Cuban Revolution. Both these
men were involved in the 1976 bombing of the Cubana Air-
lines flight 455 from Barbados to Jamaica that killed all
seventy-three on board including the Cuban Olympic fencing
team. These are well-established facts and yet they do not
have an impact on how people within the United States see
either the U.S. itself—which is seen as largely blameless—or
Cuba, which is seen largely as a dictatorship that should be
overthrown. The United States acts violently, with terrorist intent, but its reputation remains unsullied; Cuba acts to
establish the well-being of its people and to spread that policy
around the world, and it is disparaged. Consent is manufactured very effectively.

Cuba reacted to these early terrorist attacks in a way that
was unknown to the United States: the Cubans responded
by adhering to international law, namely by approaching the
United Nations Security Council in July 1960, with a request
for assistance.[40] The Cuban government provided the UN

with records of the bombings, showed the registration numbers of the aircraft, named the pilots, and provided details
of the damage. Interestingly, the Cuban government sought
to resolve this conflict by diplomatic means. These records
of the details are now buried in the United Nations system.
The United Nations Security Council responded by urging
the two countries to "refrain from any action which might
increase the existing tensions between Cuba and the United States of America." The UN said that this matter would
be better resolved at the Organization of American States
(OAS). When the U.S. National Security Council gathered a
few days later, Secretary of State John Foster Dulles said that
"the calling of the UN Security Council into session to hear
the Cuban charges had startled and disturbed Latin American Governments. Many of them were being driven away
from their previous attitude of aloofness. They would prefer
that the question of Cuba be handled in the OAS rather in
the UN."[41] On August 8, 1960, the U.S. ambassador to the
UN Henry Cabot Lodge Jr. gave the UN his "assurance [that]
the United States has no aggressive purpose against Cuba," a
statement that seems quaint given the record of U.S. aggression against Cuba (and his own president's March decision to

overthrow the Cuban government). Lodge's statement to the UN suggested that "the proper forum for the discussion of any controversies between the Government of Cuba and the governments of the American Republics is the Organization of American States."[42]

The reference to the OAS—set up with Cuba as a founding member in 1948—is interesting. The OAS, from its first meeting in Bogotá, Colombia, was intended to be Washington's instrument to fight against communism in the hemisphere. U.S. Secretary of State George Marshall stayed at the conference and indeed in Bogotá for only as long as it took for him to force the other representatives to agree to the resolution on "the Preservation and Defense of Democracy in America," which claimed that the "anti-democratic nature" of communism made it "incompatible with the concept of American freedom, which rests upon two undeniable postulates: the dignity of man as an individual and the sovereignty of the nation as a state." These phrases are comical. The coup in Guatemala in 1954 put paid to their sanctimoniousness, and the attempt to undermine the sovereignty of Cuba after 1959 hardly burnished the liberal credentials of the OAS. To suggest that the OAS—whose mandate was to snuff out

51

communism—was the legitimate place for a communist government to take its grievances showed the lack of seriousness and sincerity of the U.S. government toward Cuba's attempt to use international law to settle its dispute with the United States. Washington wanted to overthrow the Cuban Revolution and it used every means—covert and overt—to do so, including armed action. And it ran a diplomatic and information campaign to obscure its own actions and to paint Cuba—because of the communist process on the island—as the villain.

A Black Operation

Eisenhower's March 1960 directive said that the CIA operation against Cuba must be "in such a manner as to avoid any appearance of U.S. intervention."[43] This was so because of the anticipated reaction in Latin America, which would have been very much against any U.S. regime change in Cuba. That is why a pretext needed to be created to build legitimacy for the U.S. project. The Guatemala case from 1954 was instructive for the U.S. government.

President Arbenz of Guatemala knew that if he was to defend himself from a U.S. invasion or even a coup attempt, he would need to modernize his army. In 1953, Arbenz sought to get arms from Latin America (Argentina and Mexico) as well as Western Europe (Great Britain and Italy), but the U.S. blockade of his country prevented him from getting access to weapons from reliable Western suppliers. This forced Arbenz to procure arms from Czechoslovakia, a country that at that time was part of the Communist state system of Eastern Europe. When a Swedish ship, the *Alfhem*, arrived in Puerto Barrios (Guatemala) with weapons from Czechoslovakia, the CIA was jubilant. The next day, Allen Dulles told the Intelligence Advisory Committee that with these weapons Arbenz could invade all of Central America, including threaten the Panama Canal (none of which was true, since the shipment contained weapons that would only have been useful to defend Guatemala's borders). On May 17, John Foster Dulles circulated a U.S. State Department memorandum that exaggerated the entire shipment, saying that this was part of a Soviet plan to annex the Americas. This provided the fig leaf for the coup.[44] A similar fig leaf was sought for Cuba.

*The most striking fact about U.S. policy toward Cuba
has been the astonishing frenzy and hysteria. It's the
emotional content that is quite remarkable, starting
right from the beginning when the Batista dictatorship
was overthrown in January 1959. By March, the
National Security Council of the United States started to
consider means to institute regime change immediately.*

Britain had agreed to provide arms to the Cuban Revolution. The United States intervened—via CIA chief Allen Dulles—to stop the British from making any such deal with the Cubans. Dulles's "main reason," the British ambassador Alfred Fordham told London, "was that this might lead the Cubans to ask for Soviet or Soviet bloc arms."[45] Such a move, Dulles noted, "would have a tremendous effect" and would allow Washington to portray Cuba as a security threat to the hemisphere, following the script that had worked so well in Guatemala. Kennedy's close adviser the liberal scholar Arthur Schlesinger was not far from Dulles's schemes. He suggested that it would be good for the United States to trap Castro in some action that could be used as a pretext for invasion, writing the following in a memorandum to Kennedy on February 11, 1961.

Would it not be possible to induce Castro to take offensive action first? He has already launched expeditions against Panama and against the Dominican Republic. One can conceive a black operation in, say, Haiti, which might in time lure Castro into sending a few boatloads of men on to a Haitian beach in what could be portrayed as an effort to overthrow the Haitian regime. If only Castro could be induced to commit an offensive act, then the moral issue would be clouded, and the anti-U.S. campaign would be hobbled from the start.[46]

Schlesinger refers here to the government of François "Papa Doc" Duvalier, who had come to power in Haiti through a coup in 1957 and whose murderous regime had the country in a grip of fear. The general orientation of Schlesinger's view is that the attempt to overthrow Duvalier's ghastly regime would be a crime, whereas backing that regime and that of Duvalier's son Jean-Claude (or "Baby Doc") till 1986 is legitimate. There was no embarrassment from the liberal to suggest something to induce the Cuban Revolution into an action that would be merely to provide the United States with the pretext for a military invasion of Cuba. That was in February 1961. A small-scale invasion was tried in April 1961 at the Bay of Pigs.

Playa Girón

In November 1998, Kennedy's secretary of defense Robert McNamara was interviewed by the National Security Archive about the Bay of Pigs invasion and its defeat by the Cuban people. The invasion, which he called a "total failure," was driven not by the antagonism of any one president (either Eisenhower or Kennedy) toward Cuba, but "it was an antagonism of the American people toward what appeared to be happening in Cuba." McNamara told the interviewer, decades after the fact and after the Soviet Union had collapsed, that what the "American people" feared was that "Cuba was under the control of the Soviets" and that "the Soviets were likely to use Cuba as a base." In fact, at the time, none of the serious assessments by U.S. intelligence suggested that Cuba was "under the control" of the Soviets, but this impression manufactured by political elites and driven by legacy media outlets remained, and still remains. There was little factual basis for it in 1959, and still none by April 1961.[47]

In the interview, McNamara recalls that the entire operation was run by the CIA, led by Richard "Dick" Bissell, one of the more storied CIA officers. "Bissell," McNamara said, "believed that the military force would be far more effective than it turned out to be. He believed that the Cuban resistance would be far less than it was. He believed that the Cuban people would rise up and welcome this expatriate Cuban force. And he believed that if those beliefs were wrong, that the expatriate Cuban force, having landed at the Bay of Pigs, could infiltrate into the mountains, and survive as a guerrilla force." It turned out that Bissell's entire analysis was flawed. In fact, by blaming Bissell, who died in 1994, McNamara was trying to exculpate, in his typical fashion, himself primarily, and then the entire U.S. establishment—few of the senior leaders having expressed any real hesitation about this operation in the documents available in the archive. None of the high officials of the Kennedy administration—except perhaps Chester Bowles—objected to this ruthless disregard for international law.

The region of the Zapata Swamp, where the Bay of Pigs is located, had an infant mortality rate of 59 per 1,000 live births before the Cuban Revolution. The population of the area, mostly engaged in subsistence fishing and in the charcoal trade, lived in great poverty. Fidel Castro had known of this area, which is just a few hours' drive outside Havana.

In 1959, Fidel spent the first Christmas after the Revolution with the newly formed cooperative of charcoal workers, listening to them talk about their problems and working with them to find a way to exit the condition of hunger, illiteracy, and ill health. A large-scale project of transformation had been set in motion a few months earlier, which drew in hundreds of very poor people into a process to lift themselves up from the wretched conditions that afflicted them. So, when the representatives of the expropriated landlords and the mafia henchmen and former police officers—Kennedy's mercenary army—tried to land at Playa Girón, the Bay of Pigs, the people of the Zapata Swamp rallied to Fidel—who hastily drove down to personally lead the fight against the invasion. It was the presence of this new dynamism—which the CIA had not been willing to see—that defeated the invasion.

On April 20, 1961, President Kennedy took to the airwaves to talk about the defeat of his endeavor "on that unhappy island." His speech is awash in ideology, reckless about the invasion and sure, despite the failure, that communist experiments or national liberation experiments were to be swept away with the debris of history. It was the United States that tried to invade Cuba, but Kennedy described the

Bay of Pigs as if this were the Cuban Revolution doing the invading. "It is not the first time that Communist tanks have rolled over gallant men and women fighting to redeem the independence of their homeland," Kennedy said, when in fact the "independence of the homeland" was being defended by the men and women of the Zapata Swamp against an invasion from Florida. Unwilling to recognize the depth of Cuban support for their new government, Kennedy yoked in the deep-seated Cold War anxiety in the United States: "The American people are not complacent about Iron Curtain tanks and planes less than 90 miles from our shores." The actual fact was that despite landing five M41 Walker Bulldog tanks taken from the U.S. Army, the counterrevolutionaries faced not "Iron Curtain planes" but Cuban Air Force T-33 Shooting Stars (made by Lockheed), B-26 Invaders (made by Douglas), and Hawker Sea Furies (made by the UK's Hawker Aircraft), as well as a handful of Soviet-made T-34 tanks that had been used in Operation Barbarossa against the Nazis in 1941.

McNamara later testified before the U.S. Senate
that the Bay of Pigs invasion was undertaken in an

atmosphere, in his words, that was almost savage. This was reflected in Kennedy's public pronouncements after the failure of Bay of Pigs. They went totally berserk. Kennedy made a speech in which he said that these sorts of socialist societies are about to be swept away with the debris of history. Only the strong can survive, so we cannot let the Cuban Revolution continue. Kennedy privately conceded that some of his associates were slightly demented on the subject of Cuba, which was pretty accurate.

Two weeks before the invasion, Undersecretary of State Chester Bowles wrote a memorandum in which he agreed with the goal of such an invasion (overthrow the Cuban Revolution) but disagreed with the methods. Two points from Bowles are worth registering. First, that by "sponsoring the Cuban operation," the United States "would be deliberately violating the fundamental obligations we assumed in the Act of Bogotá establishing the Organization of American States." Secondly, that "those most familiar with the Cuban operation seem to agree that as the venture is now planned, the chances of success are not greater than one out of three. This makes it a highly risky operation."[48] After the defeat at Playa Girón, Bowles conceded privately that there was an almost frantic reaction for an action, a totally emotional reaction, with a lack of moral integrity among the participants.

On May 2, 1961, Castro reflected at a public rally of victory on the invasion and why it had been defeated. Those who fought the invasion, he said, were the "humble children of the people" and not the "landowners, millionaires, thieves, criminals, or exploiters."

The invaders came to fight for free enterprise! Imagine, at this time for an idiot to come here to say that he fought for free enterprise! As if these people did not know what free enterprise is! It was slums, unemployment, begging. One hundred thousand families working the land to turn over 25 percent of their production to shareholders who never saw that land. How can they come to speak about free enterprise to a country where there was unemployment, illiteracy, and where one had to beg to get into a hospital? The people knew that free enterprise was social clubs, and bathing in mud for the children.

Operation Mongoose

In 1886, the Cuban plantation owners followed the example of Jamaica (1872) and Hawaii (1883) by introducing the Indian mongoose into the Cuban wild to tackle a burgeoning rat problem. The mongoose, an invasive species, took root in Cuba. Perhaps cognizant of this history, the CIA decided to name its next major attempt at regime change Operation Mongoose, set in motion on November 30, 1961, in the wake of the defeat at Playa Girón. This new terrorist operation, supervised by Robert Kennedy and run by Edward Lansdale (fresh from his murderous activities in the Philippines and Vietnam), was designed to paralyze the Cuban economy by denying it access to world markets and by conducting acts of sabotage against Cuban agriculture and industry.[49] The attacks on Cuban infrastructure (a railway bridge here, a petroleum refinery there, a powerplant, a sawmill) were scattershot, but deadly. Harvard University professor Jorge Domínguez studied the U.S. government documents on these acts of terror and found that "only once in these nearly thousand pages of documentation did a U.S. official raise something that resembled a faint moral objection to U.S.-government sponsored terrorism." In 1963, Gordon Chase of the National Security Council wrote that these sabotage raids are "haphazard and kill innocents. Inter alia, this might mean bad press in some friendly countries."[50] Bad press: that was it, not the acts themselves, but the unfriendly reaction in friendly countries.

Operation Mongoose was the centerpiece of U.S. policy toward Cuba from November 1961 to the Cuban Missile Crisis in October 1962—and indeed, under different names, for long afterward. In February 1962, Landsdale circulated a memorandum which conceded that "we know too little about the real situation inside Cuba," and yet the U.S. government was clear that it needed to overthrow the Cuban Revolution.[51] Operation Mongoose was to run in six phases, the first three being preparation, and then by August 1962 the CIA would start "guerrilla operations" that would culminate by October 1962 into "open revolt and overthrow of the Communist regime." The personnel of this operation came from the U.S. intelligence services (especially the CIA), the U.S. military forces, right-wing Cuban and other Latin American—including Puerto Rican—mercenaries, and mafia hit men (such as John "Handsome Johnny" Roselli of the Chicago Outfit). The day after Lansdale sent this memorandum to high officials of the Kennedy administration, Robert Kennedy told the Mongoose team that the covert operations against Cuba had become the highest priority of the U.S. government.[52]

On August 23, 1962, President Kennedy signed National Security Action Memorandum 181, which underscored that "there should be an organized effort to bring home to governments of our NATO allies in particular the meaning of this new evidence of Castro's subservience to the Soviets, and the urgency on their part to limit their economic cooperation with Cuba," "new evidence" that remained at the level of innuendo.[53] The memorandum also said that Operation Mongoose must "be developed with all possible speed." Terror attacks against Cuba accelerated, with a spectacular attack on August 24, 1962, by Cuban exiles of the student group DRE, who fired shells from two speedboats at a beachside hotel, Rosita De Hornedo (Hotel Sierra Maestra), in the Miramar area of Havana, with attacks on British and Cuban cargo ships, and with contamination of sugar shipments.

In May 1962, Castro and the USSR's premier Nikita Khrushchev agreed to have intermediate nuclear missiles placed in Cuba. The September 14, 1960, coup against the democratically elected government of Patrice Lumumba in the Congo, and then his subsequent assassination under the auspices of Western intelligence services (including the CIA and Belgian and British intelligence) on January 17, 1961, sent a clear message to Cuba.[54] On February 24, 1961, Cuba's foreign minister Raúl Roa met with the Soviet ambassador to Cuba Sergey Kudryavtsev and talked about the overthrow and murder of Lumumba. It was clear that the event angered the Cubans, who were "deeply offended by this crime" and would work to build support against such events among the Afro-Asian countries.[55] The Cubans, it appeared, reluctantly accepted the missiles on their island as a shield against the continuation of unprovoked U.S. attacks on Cuban infrastructure, U.S. attempts to assassinate Cuban leaders, and U.S. threats to invade the island. The Soviets, of course, had their own agenda, which included a response to the U.S. placement of Jupiter nuclear missiles in Italy and Turkey between October 1961 and August 1962. These U.S. missiles were within striking range of Soviet targets, and so the Soviets sought a way to match the threat by putting missiles within reach of the U.S. mainland.[56]

The United States tried to build consensus in Latin America

among its allied countries in the OAS against Cuba. The main argument was that Cuba was a threat to the national security of each of the countries in the hemisphere. Mexico's ambassador to the United States Antonio Carrillo Flores replied to this line of argument, "If we publicly declare that Cuba is a threat to our security, forty million Mexicans will die laughing."[57] And so would hundreds of millions of other people in Latin America, for whom Cuba had increasingly become a country to admire rather than a country to fear.

What became the Cuban Missile Crisis of October 1962 was not the origin of any confrontation. It was in fact part of a story of U.S. aggression that began in 1959 and had continued unabated. The attitude of the U.S. war planners was made quite clear by U.S. Secretary of State Dean Rusk on October 16, 1962, during the first hours of the "crisis," when he said that the United States had the right to conduct surveillance "over Cuba, and we will enforce our right to do so."[58] Kennedy agreed to end the terrorist attacks on Cuba, a decision formally transmitted within the ranks of the U.S. establishment on October 30, 1962. They went on, nonetheless. On November 8, a Cuban exile team blew up a Cuban industrial facility, which—the Cuban government alleged—killed four hundred workers.[59] The attitude of the United States government, despite modest attempts to reach out to Castro, was that its covert operations against the Cuban Revolution would go on until it had been overthrown.

Cuba had no sovereignty in the eyes of the United States, and Cuba's airspace could be violated at any time by U.S. warplanes. Cuba played no role in the Kennedy-Khrushchev agreement to remove the missiles from Cuba, with the United State agreeing to remove the Jupiter missiles from Turkey and Italy.

The threat of the Cuban Revolution was its example, an example that grew out of the stories of land distribution and distribution of national wealth for social goods, stimulated by the actual experience of producing a decent living for the people. The problem for the imperialists was that Latin America— and in fact the world—would see the developments in Cuba as far more attractive than the policies demanded by "economic liberalization" of the Act of Chapultepec. In 1964, the U.S. State Department Policy Planning Council warned that "the primary danger we face in Castro . . . is in the impact

the very existence of his regime has upon the leftist movement in many Latin American countries. . . . The simple fact
is that Castro represents a successful defiance of the United
States, a negation of our whole hemispheric policy of almost
a century and a half."[60] The dating is almost precise. It refers
to the 1823 Monroe Doctrine. The Cuban Revolution defied
the Monroe Doctrine. That word "defiance" is once more in
a U.S. document. That defiance was inexcusable.

Coups upon Coups

In 1962, President Kennedy changed the mission of the
Latin American military forces—subservient to Washington in one way or another—from "hemispheric defense,"
the orientation from World War II, to "internal security,"
a euphemism for war against the domestic enemy, namely
those who wanted to defy the Monroe Doctrine and the Latin American elites who accepted U.S. suzerainty.[61] Charles
Maechling, the head of U.S. counterinsurgency and internal
defense planning from 1961 to 1966, was rattled by the way
this policy developed in Central America in the 1980s. There
remained in Maechling's mea culpa in a *Los Angeles Times*

opinion piece in 1982 a little of the North American prej-
udices, particularly after the U.S. brutalities in its wars in
Korea and Vietnam ("The brutality of military culture in the
former Spanish colonies is almost inconceivable by Anglo-
Saxon standards"). But, despite that lack of sincerity about
routine U.S. war crimes, Maechling wrote that the senior
officers in the militaries of Central America, fully backed by
the United States and trained at the Inter-American Defense
College in Washington, had a conduct "indistinguishable
from the war criminals hanged at Nuremberg after World
War II." These men with "direct complicity" in war crimes
followed "the methods of Heinrich Himmler's extermina-
tion squads."[62]

The spate of U.S.-initiated coups that followed World War
II had a very simple two-part formula. For an example, take
the coup against the democratically elected government of
Mohammad Mosaddegh of Iran in 1953. Mosaddegh, a
moderate politician, followed public pressure to nationalize
Iran's oil sector to better use the oil revenues for the social
good. This was what outraged the multinational oil companies, particularly those domiciled in Europe and the United
States. The first part of the formula was that countries such

69

as Iran would not be permitted to exercise even a modicum of economic sovereignty, that their resources had to be placed at the disposal of the multinational firms—a formula that runs from Iran in 1953 to Chile in 1973, both coups against the Third World.[63] To replace Mosaddegh, the United States brought back the shah of Iran, whose monarchical pretensions meant that no elections would be necessary. The shah then increased Iran's military and security spending, largely to be used for "internal security," namely to crush all dissent and to prevent any social welfare provisions from creating a constituency inside the country capable of overthrowing the shah (the shah spent half of Iran's oil revenues to buy expensive weapons systems from Western arms companies).[64] Two years after the coup, Iran joined a Western-led alliance, CENTRO (Central Treaty Organization), which was West Asia's form of the North Atlantic Treaty Organization (formed in 1949). CENTRO emerged out of the Baghdad Pact of 1955, which was forged around the discourse of anticommunism. The shah's government used the fear of communism to expand its "internal security" (including the brutal SAVAK organization) and to ensure that his regime did the bidding of Washington before that of its own public.

These two parts of the coup formula—already in evidence in 1953, almost a decade before Kennedy's articulation of the "internal security" doctrine—can also be seen in different measures in other countries.

An early application of the new "internal security" line came in Brazil. Two successive administrations—of Juscelino Kubitschek (1956–1961) and of João Goulart (1961–1964)—took a hard line in negotiations with the International Monetary Fund against the conditions that the IMF tried to impose. Their position against the IMF conditionalities earned both Kubitschek and Goulart immense popularity within their country. But this adherence to democracy won these governments no friends in Washington's inner hallways. The administrations of Kennedy and Lyndon Baines Johnson used the new doctrine of "internal security" to tighten links with the Brazilian military and to hasten moves to overthrow Goulart. The day before the coup on April 1, 1964, President Johnson told Undersecretary of State George Ball, "I think we ought to take every step that we can, be prepared to do everything that we need to do." The day after the coup, which lasted twenty-one years, the United States recognized the military government. The IMF returned to Brazil, its staff now able to do whatever they wanted. Planning for the 1964 coup goes deep into the Kennedy administration. On March 7, 1963, Robert Kennedy told his brother that he felt Goulart was a "wily politician" who had put Communists in "important positions" and was giving "speeches criticizing the United States." Goulart had to be stopped. But Goulart disregarded the pressure from the United States. He said he would put in place wide-ranging agrarian reform, and he went about nationalizing the oil refineries. U.S. Ambassador Lincoln Gordon saw President Kennedy in the Oval Office on October 7, 1963, telling him that "I would not want us to close our minds to the possibility of some kind of discreet intervention which would help see the right side win."[65] The United States did more than intervene discreetly.

Kennedy's ambassador to Brazil called the 1964 coup the most important victory for freedom in the mid-twentieth century. This was the first in a series of neo-Nazi-style national security states that then spread through the hemisphere.

The United States gave enthusiastic support for the coup, while Brazil's new military leaders instituted a neo-Nazi-style national security state with torture and repression at the center. This was a dress rehearsal for what would follow across South America through Operation Condor, the "internal security" platform for the region: military coups of a harsh neo-Nazi form took place in Bolivia (1971), Uruguay (1973), Chile (1973), Peru (1975), and Argentina (1976), with Paraguay already having gone in that direction in 1954 and with Colombia convulsed by the imposition of a harsh war against the people by the oligarchy in 1964. A hideous plague of violence swept through the hemisphere. Part of it was motivated by a desire to stop the spread of a leftist wave that had begun to crest, inspired by the example of the Cuban Revolution. Coups upon coups, blood upon blood was imposed on the world to prevent the advance of anything that resembled anti-colonialism or socialism.

The Example of Haiti

In January 1963, CLR James wrote an essay called "From Toussaint L'Ouverture to Fidel Castro" that would later be published as an appendix to the reissue of his 1938 classic about the Haitian Revolution called *The Black Jacobins*. In his essay, James wrote that what took place in Haiti in 1792–1804 "reappeared in Cuba in 1958."[66] For the purpose of James's book, the linkage between the Haitian Revolution and the Cuban Revolution made sense. However, for our purposes, another comparison would be far more useful: that between the Haitian Counterrevolution of 1957 and the Cuban Revolution of 1959.

U.S. relations with Haiti go back to the days of the Haitian Revolution, when the new U.S. republic joined the European powers to prevent the victory of the rebellion of enslaved people of African descent. Haiti's successful revolution of 1804 was met with a harsh reaction from Washington, which refused to recognize Haiti till 1862 (when the imperatives of the American Civil War, 1861–1865, forced the hand of the U.S. government). South Carolina Senator Robert Hayne put it bluntly in 1824, "Our policy with regard to Hayti is plain. We never can acknowledge her independence. The peace and safety of a large part of our Union forbids us even to discuss it." Haiti was a challenge to U.S. slavery; its freedom could not be allowed. George

Washington's government sent $400,000 to support the white planters.

Demands by France that Haiti pay for its liberation escalated into preventing Haiti—like Cuba later—from becoming defiant against the imperialists and building its own sovereign political process. For the century and a half after 1804, Haiti spent 80 percent of its revenues to pay off its debt (considerable amounts to Chase Bank in New York, which bought the debt from France). Ongoing interventions eroded the Haitian Revolution's promise, particularly the intervention of U.S. troops in 1915, authorized by Woodrow Wilson, who was president of Princeton University. This intervention morphed into the occupation of Haiti till 1934, during which time Wilson's warriors—as viciously racist as his administration—murdered and destroyed, reinstituted virtual slavery, dismantled the constitutional system to turn the country into a U.S. plantation, and established the National Guards that held the country in its grip for decades afterward. "Most observers agree that the achievements of the occupation were minor," writes Haiti scholar Michel-Rolph Trouillot. "They disagree only as to the amount of damage it inflicted."[67] The occupation by the United States, reflected

Trouillot, "left the country with two poisoned gifts: a weaker civil society and a solidified state apparatus." This state apparatus crushed all dissent—the Haitian Communist Party, formed in 1934 as U.S. Marines left Port-au-Prince, was proscribed two years later.

A few weeks after François Duvalier—later known as "Papa Doc"—came to power in late 1957, U.S. Ambassador Gerald Drew wrote a note to the secretary of state in Washington.[68] The note clarified the central role of the Haitian security services—with the military at its heart. Duvalier won the election with his army's assistance and would "not long stay in office without Army support." The U.S. ambassador felt that the chief of staff General Antonio Thrasybule Kébreau,* the former head of the military junta, was exercising his rule "through personal domination of the President and his Ministers." There was no surprise that the "surface calm" in Haiti after the election was "due largely to the public's fear of the strong repressive policy of the Army to intimidate the masses and the opposition leadership. Purely political arrests and

---

* He was nicknamed General Thompson for his troop's use of the Thompson submachine gun in the June 1957 massacre in the capital city's Bel-Air, La Saline, and Saint-Martin neighborhoods.

threats of arrests continue, as do police entry and search of private homes without warrants." This was in the first weeks of Duvalier's regime, which very soon would receive aid and assistance—including diplomatic support—from the United States government.

This support for Duvalier's regime earned immediate results for the United States, as Haiti cast the decisive vote in January 1962 to expel Cuba from the Organization of American States. While Haiti was paraded by the U.S. as a "democratic" country at the UN, and where it used its credentials to remove Cuba from the OAS, the blood continued to flow inside Haiti with the full knowledge and support of Washington. In the first decade of Papa Doc's rule, Chief of Police Jean Tassy affirmed that 2,053 people were killed in the police headquarters.[69] Over the course of the rule of Papa Doc (1957–1971) and his son Jean-Claude "Baby Doc" Duvalier (1971–1986), their militia group called the Tonton Macoute participated in the killing of around 50,000 people (the name of the group comes from a Haitian story about Uncle Gunnysack—Tonton Macoute—who kidnaps children and stuffs them in a gunnysack).[70] The United States fully backed the regime of Papa Doc and Baby Doc, with the United States Agency for International Development hoping to turn Haiti into a "Taiwan of the Caribbean."[71] Haiti was the "economic miracle" of the usual sort: U.S. taxpayers funded the establishment of corporate factories and fields in Haiti, with wages at subpar levels (a decline of 56 percent of wages in the 1980s), no unions, and ample terror. And all of this happened during the time when Cuban social indicators improved dramatically.

Talk of overthrowing the Cuban Revolution—"turning that fucking island into a parking lot," as Haig said in 1981—came alongside the establishment of the permanent dictatorship in Haiti. In June 1985, when the Haitian legislature adopted a new law that required all political parties to recognize Jean-Claude Duvalier as the supreme arbiter of the nation for life, the United States was impressed. Paul Farmer, the founder of Partners in Health, remembers that he was in the U.S. embassy on July 4, 1985, when Ambassador Clayton McManaway said that this new law was "an encouraging step forward." An unnamed U.S. State Department official told Newsweek, "With all of its flaws, the Haitian government is doing what it can."[72] Haiti was doing what it can, but the Cuban Revolution had to be overthrown. In fact, it was the Haitian Counterrevolution of 1957 that was overthrown, not by an external intervention but by the Haitian people. Baby Doc fled Haiti in February 1986, overwhelmed by the *Lavalas*, the flood, that rose from the slums to overthrow the wretched U.S.-backed dictatorship.[73]

That flood brought a former priest, Jean-Bertrand Aristide, to the presidential palace in 1990–1991, who defeated a former World Bank official and the preferred candidate of Washington Marc Bazin by an overwhelming margin (67.48 percent against 14.2 percent). Aristide should be in the Guinness Book of World Records. He is the only person to our knowledge that has been removed by a coup d'état twice, once in September 1991 and again in February 2004. Washington did not like Aristide, who tried to bring some measure of sovereignty to Haiti and to improve the social conditions in the country. In February 1991, a U.S. official in Port-au-Prince reported to Washington about "surprisingly successful efforts of the Aristide government." But things fell apart, and the Haitian military moved against the civilians in September and overthrew Aristide. Caught on the horns of its own rhetoric, the U.S. government had to place an embargo on Haiti's military junta. But, as the *Miami Herald* investigation found, this embargo was completely porous. Here's the *Herald*—which directly lobbies for the maintenance of the blockade on Cuba—in its own words:

The United States failed to take many steps that it had promised to choke the flow of money and goods to the Haitian dictators and their wealthy supporters.

According to documents and interviews with federal officials, investigators and targets of the sanctions, the U.S. government:

- Never seized U.S. homes owned by coup supporters, despite a vow to the contrary.
- Eroded its own embargo by buying baseballs and black-market gasoline from alleged backers of the regime and training military men who worked for it.
- Subverted its own goals by granting embargo exemptions to U.S. companies and wealthy Haitians.
- Delayed freezing Haitian leaders' assets for almost 15 months after the coup. By that time, the Bank of Boston found only 50.71 Haitian gourdes, worth about $5.07, in the accounts of Brig. Gen. Philippe Biamby, the Haitian army's chief of staff.

To be sure, the United States did impose penalties during the Haiti embargo, which ended last week. It fined 136 embargo violators $540,000. It confiscated three weather-beaten freighters and seized shiploads of rum, perfume and motor oil smuggled through the Miami River.

But more serious complaints—such as charges that Texaco distributed tankers of fuel—were allegedly left on the back burner.[74]

Why was the embargo on Haiti not active, when it was so rigorously implemented against Cuba? Former special envoy to Haiti Lawrence Pezzullo told the *Herald* that the embargo failed due to "a lack of leadership" in the Bush and Clinton administrations. But there was no "lack of leadership" when it came to the blockade on Cuba. The leaders of the Haitian military junta enriched themselves, and many of them—when the time came—fled into exile in Miami, where an earlier military leader—Lieutenant General Prosper Avril—already lived (Philippe Biamby went to Panama).

When I went to Haiti in June 1993, before the renewed terror, people were just afraid to even talk to me, despite the presence of a well-respected person who was translating for me. The eyes of the security forces were everywhere. They intimated by their gestures more than their words. These were uniform: hunger, no work, no hope—unless, somehow, President Aristide returns, though few dare to articulate the phrase beyond hints and nods. Some do, with remarkable courage, even after police torture and the threat of worse. It is not easy to believe that such courage can long survive, even if the people do.

Three years later, after conceding its inability to manage the situation in Haiti, the U.S. government led by Clinton—and under pressure from the Black Congressional Caucus—managed to convince Aristide to return in a deal that removed the military from power but also forced Aristide to moderate his policies. He finished his term without much enthusiasm. After a stint in the opposition, Aristide returned to the presidency with a victory in 2000. Radicalized by his experiences, and seeing how Haiti's economy could not be easily shifted away from its dependent position, Aristide called for reparations from France and demanded that a greater share of the profits made by multinational corporations be distributed to Haitian workers. He was removed in a second coup not long afterward, and was forcibly taken by the United States into temporary exile in South Africa.

In May 2022, Thierry Burkard, the French ambassador in Haiti at that time, told the *New York Times* that France and the United States had orchestrated a coup against Aristide, "probably a bit" due to Aristide's demand for restitution, a demand that "would have set a precedent" for other countries.[75] Aristide's return to power in 1994 and then in 2004, though still a threat to the multinational corporations, no longer had the buoyancy it did in 1991 with the decimation of the vibrant civil movements in the coup of September 1991 and then their almost complete retreat in subsequent years due to the increasing violence and the absence of a national project. Aristide was not able to push for regulation of the mostly U.S.-based multinational corporations operations in Haiti, nor was he able to fight for better working conditions and pay for Haitian workers. The many ways in which Aristide's policies were stifled led to the terrible situation that still prevails today.

President Bill Clinton entered office with a promise to stand up for Haiti, but of course—in an act of bipartisanship—Clinton stood with the multinational corporations and the business elites in Haiti (including the military) against the majority of the Haitian people. Haiti, starving, exported food to the United States, as well as manufactured goods that were produced by workers—many of them women—who worked for 10¢ an hour (and if they did not meet stringent quotas, they were able to make only 5¢ an hour). Of Haiti's exports, 90 percent came from the apparel sector, where as Mark Weisbrot of the Center for Economic and Policy Research noted in 2015, "The biggest problem with the 'sweatshop' model in Haiti is that workers don't have collective bargaining rights" to help them secure a living wage.[76] In 2008, the U.S. Congress passed the HOPE II (Haitian Hemispheric Opportunity through Partnership Encouragement) Act, which opened the door to the dumping of U.S. agricultural goods in Haiti. This had the effect of killing off sections of the small peasantry and emphasizing the growth of the sweatshop sector—people from the displaced rural areas moved to work in the urban sweatshops for low wages and lived in substandard housing, much of it so poorly built that it collapsed in the 2010 earthquake.[77]

The Western states took advantage of the weakness of the Haitian state to import onto the island a wide range of Western NGOs, which effectively privatized all operations in the country with NGOs providing 80 percent of the public services (including 85 percent of national secondary education). While this occurred, the United States' tightened sanctions policy against Venezuela crushed the PetroCaribe scheme, which had provided Haiti with concessionary oil sales and $2 billion in profits between 2008 and 2016 (although with the Haitian state in shambles, this money vanished into the tax havens of the Caribbean).[78]

Horrendously, when Haitian lawmakers tried to increase minimum wages on the island to $5 a day, a minuscule amount, the U.S. government intervened with diplomatic pressure on behalf of the textile and apparel companies to block the bill. David Lindwall, former U.S. deputy chief of mission in Port-au-Prince, said that the Haitian attempt to raise the minimum wage "did not take economic reality into account" but was merely an attempt to appease "the unemployed and underpaid masses."[79] The bill was defeated following this U.S. government pressure. These "unemployed and underpaid masses" are punctually on the streets, unhappy with their plight.

To compare the Cuban Revolution with the Haitian Counterrevolution is instructive and painful. It is clear that if the United States had got its way by overthrowing the Cuban Revolution at any point since 1959, the fate of Cuba would mirror that of Haiti. Both countries have about the same population (11 million), although Cuba's landmass is much greater (109,880 square kilometers as opposed to 27,750 square kilometers). Cubans live ten years longer than Haitians, have a much lower infant mortality rate, have four times less of a homicide rate, and have a better overall score in the UN Development Program's Human Development Index. The price paid by the Haitian people for imperialism's success is a negative example for the Cubans, who—despite the price that they have paid due to the blockade—live with far less onerous conditions.

In his 1963 afterword, CLR James wrote, "Whatever its ultimate fate, the Cuban revolution marks the ultimate phase of a Caribbean quest for national identity. In a scattered series of disparate islands, the process consists of a series of unco-ordinated periods of drift, punctuated by spurts, leaps, and catastrophes. But the inherent movement is clear and strong." James was optimistic about Cuba, hopeful that it would suc-ceed and provide an example for the other islands.[80] Other islands have not yet taken the leap, but the rumbles under-neath the surface never cease.

What Is a Revolution?

Cuba has been under siege from the United States since 1959, with attempts, including an invasion, to overthrow the Revo-lution. In our conversations that produced this book, one of us (Noam) recounted his first trip to Cuba in 2003, when he went to speak at a Latin American Council of Social Sciences (CLACSO) conference. During several public and private conversations—including on Cuban national television and Radio Havana—with Ricardo Alarcón, at the time president of the National Assembly, Noam raised the issue of political prisoners in Cuba and of political repression in general. "I just criticized it," Noam recounted, "explained why I thought it was wrong. We discussed it quite openly. Alarcón's reaction

was sensible. Understand your position. Don't agree with it."
These are difficult debates, but there is room to have them if
there is an understanding that these debates are taking place
in the midst of a process of building a new society.[81]

———————

*Alarcón released a book of my writings that had
been published previously in the Mexican newspaper*
La Jornada. *The book had a preface by Eduardo
Galeano and Manuel Vázquez Montalbán. After the
presentation, I took questions. I talked about my
critical attitude about political repression both there
and then later on Cuban national television and on
Radio Havana. It was a perfectly polite conversation.
Can't have that on U.S. television about Julian
Assange.*

———————

A revolution is made by human beings, and human beings are
a product of their time and of their ability to build social pos-
sibilities beyond bare necessity. The Cuban Revolution, like
many of the revolutions of the modern era, took place in a
country that had been a platform for the enrichment of other
countries and for a small plantation elite whose hopes were

often vested far away from the fields that bore them their wealth. The social wealth of these colonized countries or plantation islands was taken far away and invested in Europe and the United States, leaving little for the people, many of them descendants of enslaved Africans who had never been allowed to accumulate any assets. There was wealth produced in such places, but that wealth slipped away, leaving the workers without the resources necessary to develop the world around them.

From the first days of the Cuban Revolution, it was clear that the government had to take control of the main crop (sugar) and find markets for it that would retain resources in Cuba, and to take charge of the island's infrastructure from foreign companies that had leeched whatever resources remained behind. These elementary tasks set Cuba in a direct confrontation with the United States.

It meant that the Cuban government had to spend precious resources on its military capacity, building up a new intelligence service and ensuring that fifth columns within the island were detected and removed. A country that had never enjoyed the basics of liberal democracy could not afford to adopt a system that would allow the right wing to spread lies about the Revolution's agenda and to undermine the path set for social development. This was the actual context for the creation of the Cuban Revolution, a context that requires some hard realities to be confronted. One of the hard realities of building a Revolution is what one does with people who work with counterrevolutionary forces to overthrow the process.

In this context of relative poverty and attacks from the United States, the Cuban Revolution was able to improve the basic conditions of the lives of the Cuban people, which is why the Cuban people defend their revolution so fiercely. After the Bay of Pigs invasion, Fidel argued that "the invaders came to fight for free enterprise!," which meant that they came to return Cuba to the pre-1959 condition of near-slave labor conditions, slums, and general ill-health. There was no incentive in 1962 for the masses to rise up against the Cuban Revolution, just as there is no compelling narrative today—despite the difficult conditions imposed on the island by the U.S. blockade—to rise up in large numbers and return the country to its pre-1959 situation.

The Cuban Revolution has been able to survive because of its achievements for people's lives.

Two of its most extraordinary achievements are in the fields of education and health care, which is why the various development indices (including, after 1990, the Human Development Index) show Cuba at levels that match the richer nations, such as the United States. As with many revolutions, during the process of victory in Cuba, large numbers of professionals left the country along with the elite. The Cuban government often says that half of the doctors left the island over the course of the 1960s. Nonetheless, through the largesse of the socialist state and the hard work of those medical personnel who remained, life expectancy rates rose and infant mortality rates declined. Cuba eradicated plagues of the developing countries—malaria and polio—and brought to heel the ravages of diphtheria, intestinal parasites, and tuberculosis. In Havana's Center for Genetic Engineering and Biotechnology, Dr. Merardo Pujol Ferrer said that his country has almost eradicated hepatitis B using a vaccine developed at the center. That vaccine—Herberbiovac HB—has been administered to 70 million people around the world. "We believe that this vaccine is safe and effective," he said. "It would help to eradicate hepatitis around the world, particularly in poorer countries." As conditions of basic health

91

care improved—with local clinics and doctors set up across the country—so did basic education, first for primary and then later for secondary schools and colleges. By the 1980s, all children went to school, and adult literacy rose to near 100 percent. The Cuban Literacy Campaign that began in 1960 included the work of over two hundred thousand teachers who formed the *Alfabetizadores populares* (literacy brigades) and went across the country to vitalize education.

One way that the Cuban Revolution was able to accomplish these basic standards was that the government spent more than half of its budget on health care, education, and elder care. Human needs came before any other needs. Of course, not all problems were easily solved. The taproot of wretched social inheritances (racism, machismo) is difficult to pull out of the soil of any society. Abolishing racial discrimination by law in March 1959 sent a powerful message through the country, but it would take decades to push against the deep roots of racism that were a legacy of the period of enslavement and of the gangster era that followed. The depth of experience gained by the Revolution, gradually and over time, led to the creation of the National Program against Racism and Racial Discrimination in 2019. The same limitations presented themselves for women's emancipation, and for the establishment of dignity against a range of discriminations (including against homosexuals, and later against people who identified as LGBTQ+). The government made many mistakes in these struggles, and there were deep disagreements within the ranks of the leadership that led to zigzag advancements.

Cubans in the immediate years after the Revolution inherited the worst of the prerevolutionary attitudes and policies toward gays and lesbians. In 1965, the Cuban government even instituted a policy for gays to "unlearn" behavior through sports and martial arts, with new laws passed that harshly persecuted gays and lesbians. In the 1970s, brave struggles by gays and lesbians inside Cuba and new ideas about sexuality within sections of the Cuban government pressured the authorities to begin a reconsideration of the homophobia that had prevailed. In 1981, the Cuban Ministry of Culture released a powerful text—*In Defense of Love*—which made the case for homosexuality as normal, and for the Cuban government to repeal its homophobic laws.[82] By the mid-1980s, the Cuban government began to repeal these laws, although the process continued to require struggle. By

2018, the National Assembly had legalized same-sex marriage, and in 2022 the Cuban people voted in a new Family code that offered legal recognition to unions between people of the same sex, to adoption by same-sex couples, and that allowed noncommercial surrogacy. This code is perhaps the most progressive in the entire hemisphere.[83] The journey from the horrendous repression of gays and lesbians to the present time was not accomplished without suffering and struggle.

But how does a revolution afford to make these drastic changes, given that the productive base in Cuba was unchanged from before January 1, 1959? Namely, it relied upon the export of sugar for its revenues. When the United States government prevented the purchase of sugar from Cuba, the Cuban Revolution could very well have been destroyed. The Soviet Union and the countries that participated in the Council for Mutual Economic Assistance (COMECON) stepped in by February 1960 to buy Cuba's sugar crop and provide Cuba with credits to import a range of necessities. By the late 1980s Cuba relied on the USSR for almost three-quarters of its trade, and nearly 90 percent with the COMECON countries overall.

At the Second Economic Seminar of Afro-Asian Solidarity, held in Algiers in 1965, Che Guevara acknowledged the important role of the USSR and the People's Republic of China in signing agreements "advantageous to us, by means of which we will sell five million tons of sugar at prices set above those of the so-called free world sugar market." But sale of raw materials was hardly the basis for a structural transformation. Che gave this speech at a time when dependency theory was the most powerful approach to understand underdevelopment. The theory argued that underdevelopment in the poorer nations was produced by the development of the former colonizers, who plundered wealth to build their own societies. The former colonies were integrated into a neocolonial world system that exported lower-priced raw materials and imported higher-priced finished goods. The gap between exports and imports was the terms of trade, which was always going to be adverse for the poorer nations. This was the theoretical basis for Che's remarks.

Cuba needed to industrialize to break this dependency cycle, but to do so would require capital. And here, Che laid out a plan for socialist states to provide capital not to tie the poorer countries to them but for the full development of the poorer nation. "In this way we could unleash an immense force, hidden in our continents, which have been exploited miserably but never aided in their development. We could begin a new stage of a real international division of labor, based not on the history of what has been done up to now but rather on the future history of what can be done," Che said. Three years before, on November 16, 1962, Che held a discussion with several Soviet officials (notably, Anastas Mikoyan, close confidant of Khrushchev). The transcript of their conversation reveals how both the Cubans and the Soviets tried to figure out how to conduct trade between socialist states and—under Che's pressure—how the poorer of the two countries could be given advantages for development:

> CHE GUEVARA: I would like to ask a question regarding the construction of a refinery plant. Cuban specialists recently received the Soviet project for it. When they looked it over, they saw that the cost of the work outlined in the draft is approximately twice as much as the construction costs of similar North American plants that are located in Cuba. The specialists are well aware of the costs of building North American plants, since they participated in the construction and continue to work in these plants. Also, I

know that American monopolies tend to inflate the cost of construction in underdeveloped countries, because it helps them to take out large profits in the metropolis. Therefore, the actual difference may be even greater.

ANASTAS MIKOYAN: Right now, it is difficult to answer this question. We do not have the necessary data, but we will look into this and let you know the answer. I would like to tell you, Comrade Guevara, that our design engineers often overstate the cost of the projects, and we have to be in an uncompromising struggle with them. Sometimes, we manage to reduce the initial cost by as much as 20 to 30 percent. For example, the project of the largest oil refinery in Belarus comes to mind. After a thorough review and amendment, we were able to reduce construction costs by 30 percent. Overstating the cost usually happens because a lot of support structures are included into the project, and these support structures are not always necessary. The design engineers usually place various buildings at a great distance from each other, citing fire concerns. This, in turn, lengthens the communication lines, thereby increasing their cost. When I was in Mexico, I noticed that the various service buildings of the oil companies were arranged very compactly. And rightly so, because it reduces the construction costs. And if there is a fire, it seems to me that the enterprise will burn either way. In addition, design engineers sometimes make mistakes in counting the cost of equipment, especially if it is a new model. Different kinds of mistakes can happen, too. I remember a case with an oil refinery that we were planning to build in Ethiopia. This refinery was designed to power half a million tons of oil. When the project was finished and the Ethiopians looked it over, they said that they did not like it because it cost more than similar North American projects. We studied the situation and found out that the cost of the project included expenses for construction of a power plant that was supposed to supply electricity for the plant and for a large city, as well as expenses to build a water purification plant, which was also designed to meet the utility needs of the city, and in addition there were expenditures for construction of port facilities for receiving oil. We only had to deduct these expenses from the cost of the project, and everything fell into place. The cost of our project no longer exceeded Western models. As you can see, our engineers are far from commerce, and made plant construction cost calculations based on our internal regulations. That's why I say that we need to look into the matter. I will give an order to organize a special expertise on this project in Moscow. In connection with this, I would ask you to give us precise data on the construction costs of North American plants, to facilitate the work of our experts. If our design engineers really made a mistake, we will correct them. Such a study would be useful to the Soviet Union as well. If our plants are more expensive to make, we will have to catch up. Therefore, your criticism will be beneficial to us.

CHE GUEVARA: But I didn't criticize anybody. I only made a preliminary comment on the project.

ANASTAS MIKOYAN: We do not need to be afraid of criticism. Criticism and self-criticism are at the heart of our development.[84]

From 1960 to 1991, when the USSR collapsed, Cuba was able to sell its sugar to the USSR and was able to develop some—but not sufficient—productive forces (for instance, its pharmaceutical industry). What was needed for Cuba's development was not to become autarkic, but to be rooted in a regional economic process, such as a Caribbean common market or a Latin American market, but all political attempts to develop such a project were hampered. Take, for example, the Caribbean market. In 1958, the former British colonies in the Caribbean created the West Indian Federation, which lasted only till 1962.[85] A decade later, these countries gathered again to produce not political unity but a Caribbean Community and Common Market or Caricom in 1973. Cuba was not part of Caricom (largely because it was open mostly to former colonies of Britain), although the presence of left-leaning leaders such as Michael Manley in Jamaica opened the door for possible Cuban participation. Matters went quite favorably when the New Jewel revolution took place in Grenada in 1979, because now Cuba had a willing ally in Caricom. However, in 1980, Edward Seaga replaced Manley in Jamaica and moved his country, and in effect the other Caricom states, against Cuba (in October 1981, Jamaica cut diplomatic ties with Cuba and expelled all Cuban diplomats). The possibility of building a regional Caribbean or even a Latin American economic proposal faded. The Cuban Revolution continued to invest in social development, but it was not able to develop its productive forces in such an adverse situation.

Special Period

In 1990 and 1991, the Communist state system in Eastern Europe collapsed, and eventually the USSR was dismantled. Cuba's economy went into a tailspin, as its reliance upon the USSR and the Eastern European states had become almost total. In August 1990, the Cuban government announced the Special Period in Time of Peace, creating Option Zero, which meant that the people had to prepare for zero-oil conditions. For a time, sugarcane harvests were cut by hand and farm workers returned to the use of oxen. Scholars who later studied this period found that while daily energy intake fell from 2,899 calories to 1,863 calories, the percentage of physically active adults increased from 30 percent to 67 percent.[86] But there were new opportunities as well. Richard Levins, who first went to Cuba in 1964 to study agricultural systems, notes that during the Special Period ecologists-by-conviction were joined by ecologists-by-necessity. Though the Cuban Constitution in 1975 had said that the state must protect the environment, this was not properly enacted at that time. Despite the cutting of wood for fuel out of desperation in the Special Period, the Cubans made many innovations. For instance, agroecological practices dominated in the *organopónics* and *huertos orgánicos* (urban gardens) that had become key providers of food for the cities. Forest cover increased and freon—harmful to the ozone layer—was gradually replaced by the Cuban sugarcane derivate LB-12.[87] In December 1991, Fidel went to the National Assembly to speak to the people about the difficult situation. "What can be expected of us?" he asked. "That we capitulated, run down our flags, surrender, abandon the struggle?" Someone yelled from among the lawmakers, "Never!" That was the spirit in Cuba.

The principles of survival focused the attention of the Cuban Revolution. Food was a priority, and so was maintaining the general focus on social development. Budgetary allocations—narrowed by the lack of exports and the low-price oil—remained committed to the basics of building human life. Nonetheless, the Special Period had to demand new ways of earning income, tourism being a central possibility for a small island nation with few other resources. But tourism did not come without its costs. Resources had to be diverted to build the infrastructure for visitors and dollars found their way into the economy, creating the basis for multiple forms of corruption. Jamaica Kincaid's 1988 *A Small Place* warned about the perils of tourism for her home island

Antigua, and a rich literature had already developed by the time of the Special Period that detailed the problems that reliance upon tourism for foreign exchange might bring.[88] It was a terrible choice for Cuba to have to make, but tourism seemed the only possibility at the time.

Both of us, at different times in the aftermath of the Special Period (which ended in 2000), had conversations with Fidel Castro and other Cuban officials, who were strikingly honest and clear about the problems facing their country. When Vijay met Fidel Castro in Durban (South Africa) in 2001, he remembers how Fidel became emotional when talking about the suffering of the previous decade. This conversation took place during the World Conference Against Racism, sponsored by the United Nations, amid a great contest between the U.S.-led bloc and the Global South over how to define racism and whether to allow the idea of reparations to be on the agenda. The weakness of the Global South was evident. Fidel played the role of the leader of the South at this meeting. As usual, he was buzzing with energy, wanting to talk about how the Cuban resistance in this period gave him the confidence to lead a process for the Global South in total. The Cuban people had to struggle to maintain the integrity

103

of their Revolution, to defend their process in a world that had been left adrift after the collapse of the USSR. What was memorable about his reflections was the view that the Special Period was inevitable, because it had already become clear by the mid-1980s that the USSR could not provide the economic linkages needed by Cuba. That Cuba needed to adapt to the new era was obvious, but that it must do so by being anchored in a socialist agenda was not so difficult to maintain. Fidel spoke about how development would not come with aid or tourism but needed the enhancement of Cuba's productive forces. But, if access to capital had been difficult in the time before the Special Period, it was virtually impossible in this time. To that end, Fidel emphasized that the revolutionary forces needed to provoke a battle of ideas, a revival of Marxist theory and a socialist program to ensure that there was no drift into futility in this difficult period. Revolutions are made through culture, he said, not only by force. Education had to remain a priority so that the Cuban people could scientifically build their productive base, assist others in the region to build their own social process, and hold aloft the flag for socialism.

I met Fidel in 2003. As you know, an exchange with Fidel means a lot of listening, a couple of hours of listening, which was very interesting. He had a very fertile mind and was able to cover a range of topics, whatever came to mind. I was able to make comments here and there, but generally refrained from interrupting him. He asked me specific, probing questions about several issues, including about my assessment of the American political situation. After this long conversation, Fidel addressed the CLACSO conference, where he spoke for several hours—again going over a range of intellectual ideas, eager to drive home the importance of being focused on human problems and on the destruction of nature.

Noam and I noted that Fidel had an encyclopedic nature, seeming to know something about everything. He asked questions, sometimes very specific questions, and then listened intensely to our responses. Both of us saw him speak in public and marveled at the way he treated his rallies as seminars, offering complex ideas in a clear way to millions of people. What the Western media would caricature as demagogy was seen by most Cubans as Castro's pedagogy. Fidel's speech on December 27, 1991, to the National Assembly exemplifies his style.

We have a well-analyzed and thought-out food program. That is the number one program. There are the scientific and technical programs, and all that. There are programs aimed at preventing our populace from going hungry. All our foreign trade is also directed today to getting our country the minimum amount of fuel needed or first, the necessary food, the minimum amount of fuel needed, medicines, and if possible, soap and toothpaste and those essential things for living. So our foreign trade is aiming its efforts in that direction. Another effort such as those I have mentioned are efforts to increase our income, to increase exports through new products that have potential, quite a lot of potential, and through tourism, which has quite a lot of potential, and also through other traditional products. Among other things, now we have the sugar harvest. That is one of our most difficult challenges. It brings us all together.

Now there is the planting of what are called the winter season products, the sugar harvest, and other harvests. I think it is very good that if we do not have cement or materials, there are tens of thousands of people from the Ministry of Construction now working in agriculture. I think what the Santiago residents have done is excellent. The textile factory is a magnificent example. I said that a few days ago. Wherever there is a chance, we have men and women do something useful. Of course, our standards are the most just. We do not leave a single citizen unprotected. We do not leave a single citizen, university graduate, or middle-level technician who graduates, to his fate. We do not leave anyone to their fate. No socialist country can do that. A capitalist country could not do that. Only a socialist system could do what we are doing, with this principle of distributing what we have among all of us, as in a family.

The challenges of the Special Period drew on the Revolution's unique strengths. Cuba's focus on education and health created a social fabric that remains rational and committed, where social problems must be dealt with not with demagogy but with science. For instance, when the Cuban medical establishment saw increasing rates of loneliness among older people, the solution was for the local health workers to visit them and to provide more social activities in their communities—both logical ways to deal with one of the downsides of the modern world. Cuba was able to endure the Special Period because of this rational attitude toward major political and social problems, and because the people were encouraged to participate in overcoming these problems.

At the same time, during the Special Period the exiled Cuban reactionaries in the United States—organized in the Cuban American National Foundation (CANF) and other such groupings—smelled blood in the water. CANF was not formed to assist the Cuban American community with their many problems. It was formed in 1981 to provide the Republican Party with a vehicle to get Cuban Americans to vote for Ronald Reagan. The model for CANF was the American Israel Public Affairs Committee (AIPAC), and both have since become anchors of the Republican Party. Since 1981, CANF has been a recipient of the generosity of both the Republican Party and right-wing donors, who have used it to harden the Cuban American community in Florida against the Cuban

Revolution. Their social outlook is exactly the opposite of that of the Cuban Revolution. At its toxic center is the desire for revenge against those who took "their" property as well as the desire to establish a free-market world that they could dominate. These Cuban exiled reactionaries—*gusanos* or worms, as they are often called after Fidel's speech at the second anniversary celebration of the Revolution on January 3, 1961, where he used the word—took advantage of the presence of Cuban migrants in Florida and New Jersey to drive a harsh agenda principally through three members of Congress—Senator Robert Menendez of New Jersey (now caught in a serious corruption scandal) and representatives Lincoln Díaz-Balart and Ileana Ros-Lehtinen of Florida (Ros-Lehtinen was also caught in her own corruption scandal). The deeply divided political atmosphere in the United States made Florida appear as the "battleground" state of greatest importance, which elevated the Cuban American vote, and thus the role of CANF and its leader Jorge Mas Canosa.

Both Republicans and Democrats courted that vote, bringing Cuba into the debate over the 1992 U.S. presidential elections. Before the elections, President George H.W. Bush rushed through the Cuban Democracy Act (1992, also

known as the Torricelli Act) and shortly before the legisla-
tive elections, President Bill Clinton signed the Cuban Liberty and Democratic Solidarity Act (1996, also known as the
Helms-Burton Act). The Torricelli Act forbade the subsidiar-
ies of U.S. firms from trading with Cuba, prevented ships that
had docked in a Cuban port from entering the United States,
and cut many channels for humanitarian contact between the
United States and Cuba. The law included a section known
as Track 2, which stated that the U.S. government must
open channels for a post-Communist Cuba (nothing new
here, but nonetheless now part of U.S. law). The Torricelli
Act was mostly about trade. In 1996, another election year,
the U.S. Congress—with an eager Clinton administration in
the White House—pushed through the Helms-Burton Act,
which was mostly about finance. It not only sanctioned any
U.S. firm that conducted commercial relations with Cuba,
but even ordered secondary sanctions against firms from other countries. Any negotiations with Cuba, the Helms-Burton
Act argued, had to be done only after Cuba had resolved the
dispute over property claims by those expropriated as part of
the revolutionary process. It was transparent that these two
acts were not about Cuba per se, but about the political nar-

110

cissism of U.S. elites, who were willing to tighten the screws on Cuba for their own gain. Torricelli was a liberal congressman from Florida and Clinton was the darling of the liberals; Helms was the vicious racist senator from North Carolina. Whether Republican (Bush) or Democrat (Clinton), these representatives of the U.S. political elite held in common the sadism against Cuba that has been reflected in each and every presidential administration in the United States since January 1, 1959, even when the role of the Cuban lobby was practically negligible in the 1960s and 1970s.

The general attitude toward Cuba in the U.S. establishment was laid out by Clinton's secretary of state for Cuba, Richard Nuccio, an expert on Guatemala. In an interview with the *Washington Times* (July 30, 1995) and in a speech given to the West Point Society in South Florida (September 8, 1995), Nuccio laid out the three basic elements of U.S. policy regarding Cuba during the Special Period. The first component was "the most complete economic embargo being enforced by the United States anywhere in the world," which had begun full-scale in 1961 and had been tightened by the Torricelli Act of 1992. Second, the United States government, through its own version of Track 2 diplomacy, maintained

111

contact with sections of the Cuban American population that were preparing for a post–Cuban Revolution government. Third, the U.S. government pledged to respond "in carefully calibrated ways" to "positive developments which were to happen in Cuba"—in other words, to be prepared to assist in regime change at any time. The Torricelli Act strengthened the blockade that began in 1961, and the Helms-Burton Act of 1996 established a road map for a postrevolutionary Cuba, including a pledge for a new government to restore the property of those who had seen their private wealth (land and businesses) expropriated. There was now a hardened agenda against Cuba, weakened by the fall of the USSR, and a direct statement that the United States would like to return to the situations of prerevolutionary Cuba. The attitude of the U.S. government was made clear by Senator Jesse Helms in 1995 when he put forward his bill: "Let me be clear. Whether Castro leaves Cuba in a vertical or horizontal position is up to him and the Cuban people. But he must—and will—leave Cuba."[89]

Many of the close allies of the United States—such as Canada, the European Union, Mexico, and Japan—were bewildered by the provisions in Title III of the Helms-Burton Act, which said that foreigners could be sued in U.S. courts if they violated the U.S. blockade against Cuba. This was basically an extraterritorial application of a U.S. law, which of course violated key elements of international law. The United States bureaucrats replied to these complaints by saying that the United States was within its rights under the North American Free Trade Agreement (NAFTA) and the World Trade Organization (WTO)—both of which were established in 1994. Clinton, as a compromise, said that there would be a six-month period when no lawsuits could be filed under the Helms-Burton Act.[90] In October 1996, the European Communities went to the WTO to ask for a dispute settlement panel to be created. The WTO noted of the claim: "The EC claims that U.S. trade restrictions on goods of Cuban origin, as well as the possible refusal of visas and the exclusion of non-U.S. nationals from U.S. territory, are inconsistent with the U.S. obligations under the WTO Agreement." Neither side could budge, with the United States firm on its commitments to the act and to the overthrow of the Cuban Revolution, and the Europeans and a few others upset by the extraterritorial implications of the law. In early January 1997, Clinton once more postponed the application of the law by six months.[91]

113

The European Union welcomed this step. European Commission president Jacques Santer said that while the Europeans were happy with Clinton's suspension, "we remain firmly opposed to all extraterritorial legislation, whatever its source, and will continue to defend our interests."[92] It is important to note that there was no objection to the strangulation of Cuba. Important U.S. business interests took a line against the Helms-Burton Act because they said it would hamper their ability to do business with Cuba. Five important business lobbies—National Foreign Trade Council, Organization for International Investment, U.S. Chamber of Commerce, European American Chamber of Commerce, and U.S. Council for International Business—sent Clinton a letter with their objections laid out.

> The United States' ability to benefit from the global economy is dependent on strong, stable, and reliable rules. We believe that these benefits are jeopardized by the enormous friction that will result if Title III is allowed to take effect. Some of our closest allies and most important trading partners are contemplating or have legislated countermeasures. U.S. firms will bear the brunt of these countermeasures. . . . Many of our

member companies had property in Cuba that was expropriated by the Castro regime. Yet many of these companies, con-
stituting some of the largest certified claimants, do not believe
that Title III brings them closer to a resolution of these claims.
To the contrary, Title III complicates the prospect of recovery
and threatens to deluge the federal judiciary with hundreds of
thousands of lawsuits. These companies, Title III's intended
beneficiaries, support our view that Title III should be suspended at this time. Finally, we believe that if Title III were to
become effective, it would drive a wedge between the United
States and our democratic allies that would significantly hin-
der any future multilateral efforts to encourage democracy
in Cuba.[93]

The problem for the U.S. business community was that the
Helms-Burton Act did not help their Cuban American col-
leagues from making a claim to their lost property on the
island, nor did they feel that the act would properly create
the basis for regime change in Cuba. The goal of overthrowing the Cuban Revolution was not in dispute. What was dis-
agreeable to this section of the business community was the
strategy.

Both Canada and Mexico—parties to NAFTA, to which the U.S. government appealed for fealty to the Helms-Burton Act—passed their own laws to show the absurdity of U.S. claims for restitution against Cuba. Canada's October 1996 law was comical, "An Act to amend the Foreign Extraterritorial Measures Act" (Godfrey-Milliken Bill), which demanded recompense by descendants of Loyalists who lost their property during the American Revolution of 1776. Mexico's October 1996 law, far more serious, was the Law of Protection of Commerce and Investments from Foreign Policies that Contravene International Law, which fines companies who obey another country's laws that could reduce Mexico's foreign investment or trade. These sorts of laws illustrated the frustration that many countries, even close U.S. allies such as Canada, felt with the insane U.S. policy toward Cuba.

In 1992, the Cuban representative to the United Nations, Alcibiades Hidalgo Basulto, put forward a resolution in the General Assembly called, "Necessity of ending the economic, commercial, and financial embargo imposed by the United States of America on Cuba." Hidalgo Basulto said of the blockade that it was "the most serious of the diverse forms of aggression that the United States has carried out against Cuba." In the prior three decades, he said, the blockade cost Cuba $30 billion.[94] Fifty-nine countries voted for the resolution, including Brazil, Canada, France, Indonesia, Mexico, New Zealand, Spain, and Venezuela. Seventy-nine countries—including Britain and Germany—abstained, while only three voted against it (the United States, Israel, and Romania). Each year since 1992—except 2020, during the pandemic—the United Nations General Assembly has taken up this resolution, and each year the numbers of countries voting against the United States has increased. Over the past few years, the vote has been overwhelming:

2022   185 against 2 opposed (Israel and the U.S.)

2021   184 against 2 opposed (Israel and the U.S.)

2019   187 against 3 opposed (Brazil, Israel, and the U.S.)

2018   189 against 2 opposed (Israel and the U.S.)

2017   191 against 2 opposed (Israel and the U.S.)

Out of 193 member states in the United Nations, almost all voted with Cuba against the blockade. These are landslide votes. The General Assembly vote is not legally binding. It is a moral statement. But what is extraordinary about the vote

NOAM CHOMSKY AND VIJAY PRASHAD

is that it shows the political isolation of the United States on this issue (joined only by Israel, and once by Brazil when Bolsonaro was the president). In 2016, stunningly, the United States abstained from the vote (along with Israel), largely as a way to signal the start of the "normalization" process (when President Obama started a conversation with Cuba about taking small steps on trade and tourism); but that abstention was unusual and singular.

During the discussion of the motion in 2017, Bolivia's ambassador to the United Nations Sacha Llorenti Soliz said that "the illegal blockade was a clear example of the unilateral fashion in which the United States conducts itself in the world." He said that the United States sought to "teach" lessons about democracy and human rights, while it promotes "torture and maintains clandestine jails." "They want us to believe that they are exceptional," Llorenti said. But "they are only exceptional in their prideful acts and their constant rejection of, and flagrant disrespect for, international law." This was the overall attitude in the General Assembly in 2017. And there was more agitation due to the stance taken by President Donald Trump against Cuba, calling it part of an "axis of evil" with Nicaragua and Venezuela, and vowing to overthrow the governments in all three countries. During the discussion of the 2022 vote, Cuba's minister for foreign affairs Bruno Rodríguez Parrilla (who was one when the Revolution occurred) said that 80 percent of Cuba's population was born under the blockade. In 2019, President Trump supported a policy to overthrow the governments of Cuba, Nicaragua, and Venezuela that included tightening the blockade on Cuba as well as a "maximum pressure" campaign against both Nicaragua and Venezuela. When the U.S. government escalated the blockade in 2019, Rodríguez Parrilla said, the economic damages amounted to $154.22 billion.

Both the Torricelli Act of 1992 and the Helms-Burton Act of 1996 were the prelude to far more sadistic policies enacted by the Trump administration and continued without change by the Biden administration. Designed to overthrow the Cuban Revolution during the Special Period, these policies outlasted that era. From 2003 to 2004, for instance, the administration of President George W. Bush limited contacts between Cuban Americans and their families in Cuba and reduced the amount of money that could be remitted. It hampered agricultural trade, which had been growing; set up a Commission for Assistance to a Free Cuba; disbursed more funds for regime change; and drafted a transition plan from the Cuban Revolution to a Cuba integrated into the neocolonial world system, with a neoliberal policy framework for the island itself. But there is something important to note here. When Cuba is at its weakest, such as during the Special Period (1991–2000), the United States tightens its policy framework with Cuba. The word "humanitarianism," used with great flourish from the Clinton administration onward, meant nothing in the context of U.S. policy toward Cuba. It was merely another word weaponized to hurt the Cuban people. It was precisely this misuse of the term "humanitarianism" that set in motion Fidel Castro's immense battle of ideas, great speeches made by him at the environment conference in Rio (1992) and at the racism conference in Durban (2001), which made the case that the word "human" had been emptied of content and that the forces of good in the world had to fight to revive its original meaning.

Cuba's Global Response

What was most interesting about the Cuban response to its Special Period was that it did not minimize its international policy and retreat inward. Instead, from 1959 onward, Cuba—a very small country—developed an incredible internationalist attitude and internationalist policies. Cuba became the haven of left thinkers and militants, hosting political conferences such as the Tricontinental in 1966 and conferences on film and art that pioneered the style of the "imperfect cinema."[95] Cuba, as the capital of the Third World left, welcomed artists, intellectuals, revolutionary leaders, and cadres of revolutionary organizations to share ideas and train in Havana. At the same time, Cuban doctors, engineers, military trainers, and sports trainers went to countries in Africa, Asia, and across Latin America to provide their vital assistance.

The three most important examples of the internationalism that sparkled during the Special Period are its policy toward national liberation in Africa, its policy of medical internationalism, and its policy of leadership of the Third World.

1. National liberation in Africa. In 1988, apartheid South Africa invaded Angola.[96] This act was conducted by the South African forces to defend itself, the United States government said, from "the most notorious

121

terrorist group," Nelson Mandela's African National Congress. By this period, the U.S. government—led by President Ronald Reagan—was virtually alone in its full-throated support for the apartheid regime; it even violated congressional sanctions to increase trade with its South African ally. Washington joined South Africa in providing crucial support for Jonas Savimbi's terrorist UNITA (União Nacional para a Independência Total de Angola) army in Angola, doing so even after Savimbi had been roundly defeated in a carefully monitored free election in 1992 and after apartheid South Africa withdrew its support of him. The British ambassador to Angola Marrack Goulding described Jonas Savimbi as "a monster whose lust for power had brought appalling misery to his people." A 1989 UN inquiry, through the UN Angola Verification Mission I, estimated that South African depredations led to 1.5 million deaths in neighboring countries, including Angola. Cuba intervened in 1975 with a major troop deployment on the side of the MPLA (Movimento Popular de Libertação de Angola) and South African and Namibian forces. It was this Cuban intervention, at great cost to the small island, that beat back the South African aggressors, defeating them at the Battle of Cuito Cuanavale in 1987–88, and compelling them to withdraw from illegally occupied Namibia. Later, Fidel Castro told the journalist Ignacio Ramonet about the "overwhelming victory at Cuito Cuanavale" and how this victory by the MPLA and its allies—including the Cubans—was a "catastrophic setback" to the apartheid South Africans.[97] In 2008, Namibia's president Hifikepunye Pohamba awarded Fidel Castro with the Order of the Most Ancient Welwitschia Mirabilis, his country's highest award. "We are indebted to the Cuban government and the heroic Cuban people for this support," he said, "and we shall never forget this unparalleled example of selfless internationalism.[98]

Cuba played a fundamental role in the liberation of Africa. Castro sent Cuban forces to Angola because they knew exactly how important that struggle was to the broader fight. That it was Black soldiers defeating the white god—well, that was a sociological blow of great significance and a great encouragement to the liberation forces. In fact, as soon as Nelson Mandela was released from prison, his first trip was to Havana to thank Cubans for having played this incredible role in the liberation of Africa. Interestingly, Cubans took no credit for it. They wanted the credit to be taken by the local guerrillas. There's nothing like this in history. That's an amazing example of solidarity. Helping to overthrow vicious oppression and never even taking credit for it. And, of course, for Cuba it was very costly because it led to harsher sanctions than ever before from the United States.

---

2. Medical internationalism. In 1960, the young Cuban Revolution sent a team of medical workers to assist in the aftermath of the Valdivia earthquake in Chile. It was the start of a monumental process of sending medical teams to crisis zones (such as after catastrophic earthquakes and epidemics) and into war zones (as in Algeria in 1963). In 1998, in the midst of the Special Period, Cuba established the Escuela Latinoamericana de Medicina (ELAM), the medical school of Latin America,

where tens of thousands of students came from across the region—including the United States—to train as primary health care physicians (in line with the 1978 World Health Organization's Declaration of Alma-Ata). Seven years later, in 2005, Fidel Castro brought Cuba's medical volunteers together and formed them into the Contingente Internacional de médicos especializados en situaciones de desastre y graves epidemics, also called the Henry Reeve Brigade after a U.S. soldier who joined the Cuban fight for freedom and was killed in Yaguaramas (Cuba) in 1876. This brigade has traveled across the world, to more than fifty countries, including providing crucial support in COVID-19 hot wards during the pandemic. The United States government, embarrassed by the immense support given to Cuba for its "selfless internationalism," argued—against the facts—that Cuba "trafficked" doctors for gain ("forced labor," said the U.S. Congressional Research Service in its *Trafficking in Persons Report 2019*). The pressure from the United States was so great that the UN Human Rights Council opened an investigation, putting Urmila Bhoola (UN special rapporteur on contemporary forms

125

of slavery) and Maria Grazia Giammarinaro (UN special rapporteur on trafficking in persons) on the case. Of course, they found nothing, because there was nothing to find. The Cuban doctors went around the world to heal because they have developed an enormous sense of internationalism in their practice. When U.S. Secretary of State Mike Pompeo asked "host countries to end contractual agreements with the Castro regime" in early 2020, Brazil, Bolivia, and Ecuador—all countries at that time with right-wing governments—expelled the Cuban doctors. This was a catastrophic decision as the pandemic unfolded, leading in Brazil to excess mortality far greater than in other countries in the region. After left-leaning governments returned in Bolivia (in November 2020) and in Brazil (January 2023), so did the Cuban doctors. Little wonder that there has been a sustained campaign to ask the Nobel Committee to honor itself by giving the Cuban doctors the Peace Prize.

———————

Cuban doctors don't go to the wealthy cities. They go off into rural areas, to the most difficult areas where

*there's no medical provision, to these areas where
there is the most need for them. The domestic medical
professionals in many of these countries do not want
to go there, so they often resent and sometimes admire
the Cuban doctors. I've seen that firsthand—the Cuban
doctors working hard to establish rural health care in
very poor countries. The United States has tried hard to
prevent this.*

---

3. Cuban leadership in the Third World. In 1992, Castro went to the UN Conference on Environment and
   Development in Rio de Janeiro and—as he often
   did—helped stiffen the weak backbone of the developing countries. It was through Castro's insistence that
   many of the developing states stood firm to defend
   the formula of "common and differentiated responsi-
   bilities," which means that environmental destruction
   is commonly experienced around the world but that
   responsibility for it has to be vested with the old co-
   lonial powers, now the leading capitalist states. His
   speech at Rio began in an epic Fidel style: "An important biological species is at risk of disappearing due

to the rapid and progressive liquidation of its natural living conditions: man." Fidel's answer to the crisis was that we work to "make human life more rational." This meant taking the following steps: "Apply a fair international economic order. Use all the science necessary for sustained development without pollution. Pay the ecological debt and not the foreign debt. Hunger disappears and not man. When the supposed threats of communism have disappeared and there are no longer any pretexts for cold wars, arms races, and military spending, what is it that prevents immediately devoting those resources to promoting the development of the Third World and combating the threat of ecological destruction of the planet?" This vision by Fidel would be taken by Cuban officials from one international platform to another, with Cuba building on its leadership of the Non-Aligned Movement (it was a founding member in 1961 and hosted the NAM meetings in 1979 and in 2006) and in the G-77. When many world leaders seemed to have given up before the all-powerful United States and accepted that the "unipolar moment" was permanent, the Cubans resisted, and their resistance gave others strength. Despite the perils posed during the Special Period, the Cuban Revolution did not buckle. Castro, representing that Revolution, provided leadership where leadership in the Global South was sorely lacking. At the World Conference Against Racism in Durban, South Africa, in August 2001, Castro was the only world leader that we watched get a standing ovation in both the governmental and nongovernmental assemblies. His moral conviction was greatly appreciated at a time of weakness.

In 2000, the Special Period formally ended. One of the factors that allowed the Cubans to draw down the flag of distress was that new developments in Latin America changed the balance of forces. The election victory of Hugo Chávez in Venezuela in 1998 began an electoral process that swept through Argentina (2003), Brazil (2003), Uruguay (2005), Bolivia (2006), Honduras (2006), Ecuador (2007), Nicaragua (2007), and Paraguay (2008). It helped Latin America in this decade that the United States had become embroiled in the intractable War on Terror; in the midst of those wars

129

of mass distraction, Latin America declared its independence from the Monroe Doctrine. These new governments created platforms—such as the 2004 Bolivarian Alliance of the Americas (ALBA) and the 2010 Community of Latin American and Caribbean States (CELAC)—that denied a role for the United States in the region. A burst of Venezuelan investment and cut-price oil extended the life of the Cuban economy. In December 1994, four years before he won the election in Venezuela, Chávez spoke at the University of Havana alongside Fidel, the first time they had met. "Cuba is a bastion of Latin American dignity," Chávez said. "So as such we have to look at it, as such we have to follow it, as such we have to feed it." Cuba, in other words, was both model and inspiration. But the Cuban Revolution also needed to be sustained for the sake of a revolutionary project for the hemisphere. The closeness of Cuba and Venezuela, and later some of the other countries through the ALBA platform, not only provided support for the Cuban economy—which started to grow above 10 percent per year—but also allowed the message of the Cuban Revolution to be amplified across the world through these new developments, this "pink tide," as it was called.

Madman Theory

In 1995, under the leadership of President Clinton, the U.S. Strategic Command (STRATCOM) drafted a strange text, little remarked upon at that time, called "Essentials of Post–Cold War Deterrence." The old deterrence policy required a bipolar world—the Soviets on one side, the United States on the other. In this bipolar world, both actors were seen as rational, and stability could be imagined if each side understood that the other could destroy it if anyone decided to act recklessly. That was the basic outlook of Cold War deterrence. But with the Soviet Union no longer in place, what kind of deterrence would be possible? Or would deterrence be necessary when only one power—the United States—had the capacity to destroy the world? The STRATCOM document is one of the most horrifying documents we have ever read.

I wrote about this document. You can find commentary on it in my books, but nowhere else. Effectively it says that the United States must adopt a national persona of irrationality and vindictiveness because that will terrify our enemies. We must continue to make nuclear weapons and to cast a shadow over other countries that

*will think we are so irrational and vindictive that we
must just act out of rage. This is the official madman
theory policy. It is not something that you'll read in any
official biography of a president. I've been screaming
about this from the depth of my lungs for thirty years.*

———————

Every self-respecting U.S. president must have a doctrine.
The Clinton Doctrine was encapsulated in the slogan
"multilateral when we can, unilateral when we must." The
phrase "when we must" was clarified by the use of the word
"exerting" in the December 1999 *National Security Strategy for a New Century*: "By exerting our leadership abroad,
we have deterred aggression, fostered the resolution of con-
flicts, enhanced regional cooperation, strengthened democra-
cies, stopped human rights abuses, opened foreign markets
and tackled global problems such as preventing the spread
of weapons of mass destruction, protected the environment,
and combated international corruption." "Essentials of Post–
Cold War Deterrence" was issued by STRATCOM in 1995,
well after the Soviet Union had collapsed and as Clinton
extended President George H.W. Bush's program of expanding NATO to the east in violation of promises made to Soviet

premier Mikhail Gorbachev—with reverberations to the present. (U.S. Secretary of State James Baker and Soviet foreign minister Eduard Shevardnadze signed an agreement at the time of the unification of Germany in 1990, "There would, of course, have to be iron-clad guarantees that NATO's jurisdiction or forces would not move eastward. And this would have to be done in a manner that would satisfy Germany's neighbours to the east. . . . We understand the need for assurances to the countries in the East. If we maintain a presence in a Germany that is a part of NATO, there would be no extension of NATO's jurisdiction for forces of NATO one inch to the east.") The STRATCOM study was concerned with "the role of nuclear weapons in the post–Cold War era." A central conclusion: that the United States must maintain the right to launch a first strike, even against nonnuclear states. Furthermore, nuclear weapons must always be at the ready because they "cast a shadow over any crisis or conflict." These nuclear weapons, that is, were constantly being used, just as you're using a gun if you aim but don't fire one while robbing a store (a point that the late Daniel Ellsberg repeatedly stressed). STRATCOM went on to advise that "planners should not be too rational about determining . . .

what the opponent values the most." Everything should simply be targeted. "[I]t hurts to portray ourselves as too fully rational and cool-headed. . . . That the U.S. may become irrational and vindictive if its vital interests are attacked should be a part of the national persona we project." It is "beneficial [for our strategic posture] if some elements may appear to be potentially 'out of control,'" thus posing a constant threat of nuclear attack—a severe violation of the UN Charter, if anyone cares (all of chapter VII of the charter would scream in indignation, if the charter could only scream!). In other words, the United States—in this unipolar landscape—must act as the madman.

Everything means the opposite of what it says. Deterrence means that the U.S. offensive stance should primarily be based on nuclear weapons because they're so destructive and terrifying. And furthermore, just the possession of massive nuclear forces casts a shadow over any international conflict; people are frightened of the United States because Washington has this overwhelming force. The United States cultivates this national persona of irrationality with forces out of control so that it can really terrify everybody and get what it wants. Furthermore, other people are right to be terrified because the U.S. is going to have these nuclear weapons right in front of them, which will blow them all up—in fact, blow the whole world up.

In 1947, Senator Arthur Vandenberg counseled President Harry S. Truman about how best to increase aid to right-wing governments in the anticommunist Cold War. "Mr. President, the only way you are ever going to get this is to make a speech and scare the hell out of the country."[99] The "this" here was to increase U.S. aid to the right-wing governments in Greece and Turkey to battle their communist insurgencies, fierce in Greece with the formation of the communist-led Provisional Democratic Government (built during the civil war of 1946–1949). The United States decided to intervene directly in these countries—having already intervened in the elections of France (1945) and soon to intervene in Italy (1948)—to undermine the surging communist support. The United States planned to transfer $400 million to these governments as part of the new Truman Doctrine (1947), a policy for the U.S. to openly provide support to governments against communist forces—now called authoritarian or terrorist. The U.S. increased its own military budget and overseas military aid to right-wing and liberal governments in this process. Within the United States itself there was a reason for this ballooning of military spending, which was partly a way for the U.S. capitalist state to conduct countercyclical spending by putting government money into the military and not into the social arena (education, health, housing)—a policy known as "military Keynesianism." The enormous U.S. military was used in a general way to attack the growth of the left, including national liberation struggles. It was in this context that Cuba would find itself, with the madman or the Godfather eager to smash the Cuban Revolution to prevent its defiance and to prevent its example.

From 1959, twelve years after the Truman Doctrine was adopted, the United States attacked Cuba as part of this broad attack on all communist forces around the world. In 1979, during the Carter administration, the United States designated Iraq, Libya, South Yemen, and Syria as "state sponsors of terrorism" and developed a list that was announced each year. Cuba was not on the first list but was placed on it in 1982 during the Reagan administration, and remained on the list till 2015, when it was removed as part of Obama's process of "normalization." The designation has immense consequences: there are sanctions (including against basic financial operations through the dollar-denominated world financial system—such as the transfer of remittances to Cuba and the payment of bills by Cuban companies for imported goods) and there are implications for state immunity (state sovereignty is essentially withdrawn and nationals of the country can face legal challenges by U.S. nationals in the U.S. court system). The use of this list is entirely political. For instance, Iraq was placed on the list in 1979 but removed from it in 1982, when Cuba was added to the list. Why was Iraq removed from the list in 1982? The United States removed Iraq (led by Saddam Hussein) from the terrorist list because the United States (under Reagan) wanted to support its friend Saddam, and his attacks on Iran and the Iraqi people—including poisoning tens of thousands of Iraqis with chemical warfare. Iraq was returned to the list in 1990, when Saddam became a liability (and after the war against Iran was over; it was a very transparent demonstration that the list is not about principles but power). When the Cold War ended, there was some expectation that these instruments might be dismantled, but in fact they were strengthened. In 1994, U.S. National Security Advisor Anthony Lake wrote an article in *Foreign Affairs* that labeled five countries

137

as "rogue states"—Cuba, the Democratic People's Republic of Korea, Iran, Iraq, and Libya.[100]

Central to the arsenal of the U.S. government when dealing with countries that it sees as adversaries is the Office of Foreign Assets Control (OFAC), set up in December 1950, and located in the U.S. Treasury Department. The main reason to set up OFAC—taking over from the Office of Foreign Funds Control, set up in 1940—was to block all Chinese and North Korean assets after China entered the war in Korea. Cuba, after 1959, faced the brunt of OFAC checks and investigations. In 2004, OFAC informed the U.S. Congress that of its 120 employees, four had been tracking the finances of Osama bin Laden and Saddam Hussein, while almost two dozen of them were tasked with the enforcement of the blockade of Cuba.[101] From 1990 to 2003, OFAC conducted ninety-three terrorism-related investigations that netted $9,000 in fines, and 11,000 Cuba-related investigations that led to $8 million in fines. The revelations received silent treatment in the United States, though Senator Max Baucus (Democrat from Montana) joined with four other senators to write to President George W. Bush to contest the request for more resources from OFAC to squeeze Cuba.

Senator Baucus's statement, now largely forgotten, is worth recounting here:

> At a time when the United States faces very real terrorist threats in the Middle East and elsewhere, the Administration's absurd and increasingly bizarre obsession with Cuba is more than just a shame, it's a dangerous diversion from reality. And now the Administration's Commission for Assistance to a Free Cuba has decided that even more of our precious resources should be dedicated to cracking down on the Cuban people and Cuban government—despite the obvious failure of 40 years of embargo. From what I've seen, the Commission wants to restrict the small remittances that Cuban-Americans are allowed to send their families on the island and limit how often they may travel to visit. This is clearly an attack on the Cuban people and a further outrageous waste of OFAC's time and resources. I think this Commission is a sham, and I urge the President to rethink his support of the Commission's proposals.[102]

But the "bizarre obsession" was not necessarily a "dangerous diversion from reality," if the entire point of the U.S.

139

government was to ensure that no power—neither big nor small—felt that it could defy the United States. If the goal is to prevent defiance, then the OFAC investigations, the placement on the U.S. State Sponsors of Terrorism list, and the financing of counterrevolutionary terrorist groups (including, at one time, the forces that became al-Qaeda) were rational— but rational ony in a madman type of way.

Normalization

Months after the Cuban Revolution, the United States and its allies in Latin America worked hard to isolate Cuba. The U.S. began a formal blockade of Cuba in January 1961, and in January 1962 Cuba was expelled from the Organization of American States. At no point in its post-1959 history did Cuba resist opening channels to the United States and finding ways to normalize diplomacy. It was the United States that at each moment shut the door to normalization, although Washington used the possibility of normalization as part of its range of instruments to attempt the overthrow of the Cuban Revolution. Left-wing forces within the United States fought for normal relations with Cuba, but they remained a minority. The U.S. corporate community—which has real power—worked with the U.S. government from 1959 to 1991 to overthrow the Cuban Revolution. During the Special Period, major U.S. corporations—including many associated with the U.S.-Cuba Trade and Economic Council—made significant moves to open trade with what they considered to be a weakened Cuba. In 1994 and 1995, hundreds of corporate executives traveled to Cuba, including from large corporations such as AT&T, Chase Manhattan, Dow, Eli Lilly, General Motors, Merck, Radisson, and Texaco.[103] They preferred a Free Trade Area rather than a Five-Year Plan. The role of the corporation sector, particularly in certain areas such as pharmaceuticals and agrobusiness, was key for the pressure on the U.S. political class regarding normalization of U.S.-Cuba diplomatic relations.

U.S. politics is confounded by an accordion effect, with the Republicans and Democrats going back and forth over the decades with a similar orientation toward the world but with different strategies and different moods. On Cuba, in the early years, there was almost no difference between the Republicans (Eisenhower, Nixon, Ford, Reagan, George H.W. Bush, George W. Bush) and the Democrats (Kennedy, Johnson,

Carter, Clinton)—each of these presidents, despite their over-all attitude to the world, were committed to the overthrow of the Cuban Revolution using all the instruments available to the U.S. government. Things seemed to change a little dur-ing the Clinton administration, when Clinton seemed to do a dance between the Cuban American hard right and the gov-ernment in Cuba. But, in sum, Clinton's approach—with the Helms-Burton Act of 1996 as the pendant—was no different than the Kennedy approach of invasions and economic war.

George W. Bush began his term as president with little interest in Cuba, although his administration reflexively lifted restrictions on travel to Cuba. Before long, the Global War on Terror eclipsed all else and the only point of interest with Cuba was the U.S. base at Guantánamo Bay. In 2003, Bush set up the Commission for Assistance to a Free Cuba, which could very well have been a holdover from the Reagan administration. The commission followed the Helms-Burton Act, releasing a five-hundred-page report that specifically sought to prevent the Cuban Revolution from surviving after Fidel Castro with the creation of a new "transition coordina-tor" in the State Department to monitor Cuban compliance with the new rules set out in the report.

Obama appeared on the scene with promises to change the temperature of U.S. foreign policy, although very quickly his commitment to the status quo and his skill at Clinton's form of triangulation put an end to those promises. At the Summit of the Americas at Port of Spain (Trinidad and Tobago) in April 2009, months after taking office, Obama said, "The United States seeks a new beginning with Cuba." This statement came a day after Cuba's Raúl Castro said that his government was willing to talk about anything and everything, an open hand gesture that would normally have been dismissed.[104] Debates in Washington, and Obama's own ability to say things and do the opposite, stalled any progress on U.S.-Cuban relations. Obama returned to the theme in 2013, at a fundraising event in the home of CANF's Jorge Mas Santos in Miami. "Keep in mind that when Castro came to power," Obama said, "I was just born." He was born in 1961. "The notion that the same policies that we put in place in 1961 would somehow still be effective as they are today in the age of the Internet, Google, and world travel, doesn't make sense."[105] Pressure from the business community was paramount in the Obama White House on this issue. And despite the backing of people like Jorge Mas Santos to effect some changes, Obama faced serious intractable forces in Congress and among sections of the Cuban American right.

On December 17, 2014, Obama announced the "normalization" policy, which opened the door to a new kind of relationship with Cuba.

Rather than pursue the policy of suffocation for regime change, the Obama administration said quite forthrightly that it would like to try the weapon of consumerism and the values of capitalism to erode the Cuban Revolution. But the real driver behind this policy were the quite forceful needs of the U.S. business community. As Obama said when he announced the new policy in 2014:

> I believe that American businesses should not be put at a disadvantage, and that increased commerce is good for Americans and for Cubans. So, we will facilitate authorized transactions between the United States and Cuba. U.S. financial institutions will be allowed to open accounts at Cuban financial institutions. And it will be easier for U.S. exporters to sell goods in Cuba.[106]

Sections of the U.S. business community had complained about the advantages delivered to Canadian, European, and

Latin American companies for access to the Cuban market. They lobbied for entry into Cuba's high-end pharmaceutical industry, for instance. Obama's reforms allowed a range of firms—such as AirBnB and Verizon—to begin to operate in the Cuban market, to provide services to both tourists and Cubans.

Despite these limits set by the legacy of U.S. policy, by the nastiness of the U.S. elite, by the desires of the U.S. corporate system, the "normalization" with Cuba lessened the worst of the pressure on the Cuban people, such as by allowing freer access to remittances from overseas Cubans to their families in Cuba and by allowing the Cuban government to import key machinery to upgrade the basic infrastructure of the country. Indeed, in his announcement, Obama instructed Secretary of State John Kerry to investigate Cuba's place since 1982 on the U.S. State Sponsors of Terrorism list, a notification with terrible adverse consequences (in May 2015, Obama removed Cuba from the list). In March 2016, Obama traveled to Cuba, the first visit by a U.S. president since the Revolution, where he said, "I have come here to bury the last remnant of the Cold War in the Americas. I have come here to extend the hand of friendship to the Cuban people."

Obama's statements were interesting. He said he wanted to bring democracy to Cuba by peaceful means, by normalizing relations. In the back of his mind, he was thinking about a color revolution, to induce Cubans to become obsessed with consumption of U.S. goods and services. Get the kids hooked on, you know, Instagram or whatever it is. Nice sneakers that they can buy. Maybe bring "democracy" that way to Cuba instead of bringing "democracy" to Cuba by slaughtering and starving the Cubans. This would gradually bring Cubans into the U.S. orbit. This is not a change of strategy, but a change of tactics. It was the same with Carter. It has been the constant strategy of the U.S. to integrate Cuba with the United States. To make it like Central America or other parts of the Caribbean. If terror didn't work, then try sanctions. If sanctions don't work, try harsher sanctions. Straight invasion is not going to work. It's beyond that point. The U.S. is no longer capable of that. So it uses other devices, such as sanctions, which may work. It's kind of amazing that Cuba has even survived.

Obama's normalization policy was not comprehensive. The U.S. president cannot undermine U.S. law (the Helms-Burton Act, for instance). Congress was unwilling to repeal the laws that enforce the embargo (particularly the Trading with the Enemy Act of 1917, the Foreign Assistance Act of 1961, the Cuban Assets Control Regulations of 1963, the Cuban Democracy Act of 1992, the Helms-Burton Act of 1996, and the Trade Sanction Reform and Export Enhancement Act of 2000). This meant that Obama had to renew sanctions in September 2015 while he pushed various federal agencies to loosen their rules. Banks and financial institutions continued to be fined despite the assurances of normalization, and it remained difficult for Cuban institutions to conduct normal commercial business. The Cuban government argued that from April 2015 to April 2016, during the high point of the "normalization" campaign, the blockade cost Cuba $41 billion (at a time when Cuba's current account surplus was $1.9 billion). In January 2015, Castro wrote in *Granma* that he does not "trust the United States' policies," which was a fair assessment given Obama's promises, the underlying reasons for the "normalization," and the intractability of the U.S. Congress.

In one of his last pieces in *Granma*, Castro wrote of the "uncertain destiny of the human species." He worried about the ascension of Trump and other like-minded politicians, but he also worried about the policies of Obama. None portend well for the planet. Trump and Obama might appear different, Castro suggested, but they are united in their fealty to the United States, the "most powerful imperialist country that has ever existed." Both Trump and Obama, wrote the old revolutionary on his deathbed, "will have to be given a medal of clay." The Earth cannot afford to give them anything else. They have already laid claim to everything.

The Tale of Two Islands

In 2017, Hurricane Maria struck Cuba and Puerto Rico very hard. Both islands experienced severe disruption. But Cuba—despite the blockade and the Trump harshness—recovered much faster than Puerto Rico, which continues to be controlled by the United States since the occupation of 1898.

The people of Puerto Rico have little democratic control of their institutions and resources. Public finances at the time of the hurricane in the island were a mess—the island overwhelmed by $120 billion in debt and pension liabilities. Payment of these debts is constitutionally mandated, with debt servicing draining the state government of the ability to move an agenda to benefit the just over three million Puerto Ricans. Half the population could not find work before the hurricane struck, with public facilities killed off as the local government throttled them of funds. No wonder, then, that protests across the island had become a normal feature of life before Hurricane Maria. One area of concern had been Puerto Rico's electricity grid. A shocking 98 percent of its electricity comes from fossil fuels. Without any local oil, gas or coal, Puerto Rico receives its fuel by ship, the people buying electricity at rates higher than paid for on the U.S. mainland. The imported fossil fuels and a centralized electricity grid left the island vulnerable to the shock of the hurricane. The grid collapsed in the hurricane, and electricity was unavailable for years. Desire to privatize the electricity company is at the top of the list of desires by the U.S. government. Naomi Klein's concept of "disaster capitalism" is made for this situation—as a disaster strikes, money is to be made by the oligarchy on the disaster, both on the defaulted bonds and on the privatization of public resources. Whatever relief was provided for the Puerto Rican people came from small-scale community organizations such as Casa Pueblo (Adjuntas), Dalma Caragena's Agriculture in Harmony with the Environment project (Orocovis), the Mutual Aid Project (Mariana), and Organización Boricuá.

Cuba, like Puerto Rico, was struck hard by Hurricanes Irma and Maria, but the situation there was utterly different. When a hurricane comes, Cuba prepares by moving its vulnerable population to safety and by detaching its already decentralized power system. The devastation is managed and the recovery is as swift as possible. It should startle the reader that even though Cuba was hit by the same hurricane, it offered to send medical personnel and electrical workers to help the people of Puerto Rico (as it had offered help to the people of New Orleans after the 2005 Hurricane Katrina, a storm that also struck Cuba with equal velocity). Cuba's people are organized into voluntary units and its infrastructure is decentralized to mirror the decentralization of governance on the island.

Pushed by the blockade and by a deep interest in sections of the Cuban Communist Party in ecological socialism, the Cubans held an ecological conference in 1980, created the

National Commission for the Protection of the Environment and the Preservation of Natural Resources, and passed Law no. 31 in 1981 to protect the environment. It was in this context that Fidel Castro made the comment at the 1992 UN Rio Conference on Environment and Development, "Tomorrow will be too late to do what we should have done a long time ago." Cuba offers a window into countrywide projects based on the principles of agroecology—urban farming with biopesticides, farmers cooperatives, ban on the construction of homes in coastal areas, and Integrated Neighborhood Transformation Workshops (TTIB) that bring together neighbors who have a range of skills to solve problems for their own localities. There are limits placed by the embargo and by history—reliance upon fossil fuels is one, while reliance upon food imports is another. But, in terms of the energy grid, after Hurricane Katrina, Cuba reformed its entire system phasing out incandescent bulbs and breaking up the energy grid. Cuba plans to have a quarter of its energy needs from renewable sources and hopes to deepen its use of renewable energy in the years to come. But the blockade does not permit Cuba to collaborate with the best technology firms or to import needed inputs to fix the problems in its electrical system.

151

In August 2022, the Cuban energy grip showed major signs of stress, with power cuts becoming part of normal life on the island (people in some provinces experienced eight hours of cuts). The explosion at the Matanzas oil storage facility left Cuba without fuel and led to the deaths of five firefighters. Mexico and Venezuela immediately dispatched firefighters and firefighting equipment to Cuba, but the United States government offered only technical advice by telephone. Hurricane Ian hit Cuba just after this, destroying 50,000 homes and 8,500 hectares of cropland in Pinar del Río.

———————

Cuba has developed a very effective system of dealing with the hurricanes that routinely strike the island, as they strike most of the Caribbean and the U.S. coastline. But this system is struggling to survive the lack of access to machinery and new technology. The U.S. has used its blockade not only to prevent relief for Cubans after the hurricanes—as Carter did, even though he provided U.S. aid to other islands—but also to use the damage done by hurricanes to hurt Cuba more. Meanwhile, after Hurricane Katrina in

2005, Fidel Castro offered to send Cuban emergency personnel to New Orleans. The Cuban detachment was at Havana airport ready to go. The Bush administration rejected it. It would make the U.S. look bad. There's destruction from a hurricane: the U.S. uses it to squeeze Cuba, while Cuba offers to send medical personnel to help Americans. You decide which is the better approach.

———————

In Puerto Rico, there is a group that call themselves the Puertopians. They are libertarian, antisocialist capitalists who want to turn Puerto Rico into their own little paradise. Their vision for Puerto Rico resembles Cuba under the control of the U.S. mafia; their utopia is Cuba, circa 1958. These Puertopians are very much like the Cuban Americans and their right-wing friends who fantasize about a postrevolutionary Cuba that will allow them to exploit the Cuban people and the country's resources for their own narrow, private gain. If these Cuban "utopians," like the Puertopians, get their way, the Cuban people will experience the kind of despair experienced by the Puerto Ricans after Hurricane Maria.

State Sponsor of Peace

It was clear that Donald Trump was going to undo the overall policy opening by Obama regarding Cuba. Just a few weeks after his election, Trump tweeted, "If Cuba is unwilling to make a better deal for the Cuban people, the Cuban/American people and the United States as a whole." It was clear that Trump meant business. He brought Mauricio Claver-Carone onto his transition team for the Treasury Department. Claver-Carone, who ran the Cuban Democracy Advocates, a right-wing advocacy group in Washington, wrote in the *Miami Herald* that "there's no longer any rational strategy behind President Obama's Cuba policy."[107] A few months into his presidency, Trump reversed many of Obama's actions regarding Cuba, and pushed hard for regime change in the service of "free enterprise."[108] Over the course of the next few years, Trump unraveled the "normalization," banning private travel to Cuba (with a few exceptions) and tightening the financial restrictions (including 243 new sanctions).

From the sewers of the national security apparatus, Trump resurrected John Bolton as the national security advisor. In George W. Bush's administration, Bolton had coined the phrase "axis of evil" in 2002 to include Iran, Iraq, and North

Korea. Now, in Trump's coterie, with eyes fixed on Latin America, Bolton gave a speech at Miami's Freedom Tower on November 1, 2018, where he unveiled the phrase "Troika of Tyranny" to refer to Cuba, Nicaragua, and Venezuela. The United States, Bolton said, "will no longer appease dictators and despots near our shores." This was effectively an act of war against these three countries, in the same way as Bolton's other trinity (axis of evil) was an act of war to extend the Global War on Terror. During the same speech, Bolton welcomed the election of Jair Bolsonaro in Brazil, a "like-minded" person. With this attitude, the Trump administration not only began to tighten the sanctions regime against these three countries, but it also edged the United States to open war against them.

The Trump attack on Cuba had very deep repercussions for Cuban families inside and outside Cuba. Western Union had played an important intermediary role to transmit remittances. In November 2020, Western Union suspended delivery of remittances and closed 407 offices on the island. This closure meant that people could not provide basic income support to their families on the island. More than half of the Cuban people had come to rely upon some kind of remittance as their main source of direct income (about 700,000 Cuban migrants out of the estimated total of 2.3 million migrants send remittances home on a regular basis).[109]

During the Obama administration, the Cuban government welcomed representatives of the Colombian government and the negotiators for the Revolutionary Armed Forces (FARC) of the two sides came to Havana to bridge their differences and try to make peace. UN Secretary-General Ban Ki-moon went to Havana for the signing ceremony, where both sides agreed to a cease-fire. "On this day," Ban said, "in a world beset by seemingly intractable wars, the peace process in Colombia delivers on a key commitment: an agreement on a cease-fire and the laying down of weapons." He congratulated the host country—Cuba—and Norway, as well as Chile and Venezuela, for devoting "considerable diplomatic skills" and accompanying the process to fruition. Cuba played a key role in bringing peace in Colombia, a country that has been wracked by a terrible civil war since 1948 that claimed the lives of hundreds of thousands of people. Trump sniffed at this deal from afar, seeing in it—rightly—the possibility that with a peace agreement the left could regroup in Colombia and defeat the grip of the right. For Trump, nothing could be done about Colombia, but Cuba needed to be punished. This revenge would wait for the final days of the Trump administration. In the last days of Trump's presidency, he returned Cuba to the U.S. State Sponsors of Terrorism (SSOT) list. This was a vindictive act. Trump said it was because Cuba played host to guerrilla groups from Colombia, notably the National Liberation Army (ELN). Cuba refused to extradite the leaders of the ELN because the Cuban government said that this would violate the protocols of the negotiations.

Cuba on the list of terror states? Cuba was put on that list in 1982. The U.S. conducted terror campaigns against Cuba, and it was Cuba that was placed on the terror list! It was for an interesting reason: there was a gap in the terrorist list. The United States had removed Iraq from the terror list because the U.S. wanted to support its friend Saddam Hussein, so that he could attack Iran after the revolution in that country in 1979. Saddam's armies used chemical weapons—supplied by the West—against Iran and against the Iraqi people.

157

*That was no longer terrorism for the U.S. He was a
great friend. He was taken off the terrorist list. Cuba
was added in to fill the gap.*

———————————

By returning Cuba to the SSOT list and by introducing 243 new sanctions, Trump hardened U.S. policy toward Cuba. The impact has been profound. U.S. firms refuse to do business with Cuba due to the fear of being hit with fines or because of criminal liabilities, while firms from other countries fear the extraterritorial capacity of the United States to hit them with fines and other punishments. Shipping companies and fuel companies decided it was easier to obey the United States than risk its wrath. The Washington Office for Latin America drafted a list of damages inflicted on Cuba following its SSOT designation, which continued into the Biden administration. One of these is the financial penalty:

As a result of the SSOT designation, banks, financial institutions, companies, and investors are hesitant to engage with Cuba—a practice known as over-compliance. Cuba's presence on the list limits private individuals from opening bank accounts abroad, using instruments for international collections and payments, accessing fintech companies and digital banking, and contracting of online servers and services. These barriers not only stifle the few avenues available for Cubans to expand private sector growth and development, which the Biden administration has committed to support, but are also an obstacle for Cubans living abroad. The SSOT designation has a chilling effect on businesses, including banking or tele-communications investments, that are crucial to promoting the type of transformation essential to expanding freedom on the island. In turn, even when direct foreign trade expands, private companies will find restrictions on the purchase of products manufactured in the U.S. and even goods produced in third countries that incorporate a high content of inputs from the U.S.[110]

Afraid that a future administration might reverse the SSOT designation, Representative Maria Salazar and Senators Rick Scott, Marco Rubio, and Ted Cruz put forward a bill into the U.S. Congress called—without blushing—"Fighting Oppression until the Reign of Castro Ends" Act (FORCE Act). This bill was put forward on March 28, 2023, when the president of Cuba was no longer a Castro but Miguel Díaz-Canel. The bill hastily went through the House Foreign Affairs Committee. It remains in process in Congress.

Failed Cuba Policy

In March 2020, while a candidate for the U.S. presidency, Joe Biden said that he would "promptly reverse the failed Trump policies that have inflicted harm on the Cuban people." He strongly criticized Trump's "harmful" policies and promised a new policy orientation. In February 2021, after Biden entered the White House, his senior advisor Juan González said that the United States would soon lift remittance and travel restrictions as well as review the situation of the U.S. embassy in Havana. But then in March, White House press secretary Jen Psaki said, "A Cuba policy shift is not currently among President Biden's top priorities." But neither Psaki nor Biden explained this policy shift. That lack of any public acknowledgment of the violation of his promises and of the maintenance of "the failed Trump policies" defined Biden's stance toward Cuba. Many options existed for Biden to shift—even slightly—from the Trump agenda. He could have softened the view that Cuba was against U.S. antiterrorism efforts or that Cuba had allowed religious freedom. None of these small changes were allowed.

In July 2021, Cuba experienced a set of protests from people expressing their frustration with shortages of goods and a recent spike of COVID-19 infections. Within hours of receiving the news that the protests had emerged, President Miguel Díaz-Canel went into the streets of San Antonio de los Baños, south of Havana, to march with the protesters. Díaz-Canel and his government reminded the eleven million Cubans that the country has suffered greatly from the six-decade-long illegal U.S. blockade, that it was in the grip of Trump's 243 additional coercive measures, and that it will fight off the twin problems of COVID-19 and a debt crisis with its characteristic resolve. Nonetheless, a malicious social media campaign attempted to use these protests as a sign that the government of Díaz-Canel and the Cuban Revolution should be overthrown. It was confirmed a few days later that this campaign was run from Miami, Florida, in the United States. From Washington, DC, the drums of regime change sounded loudly. But they have not found much of an echo in Cuba. Cuba has its own revolutionary rhythms. On July 17, tens of thousands of Cubans took to the streets to defend their Revolution and demand an end to the U.S. blockade. President Díaz-Canel said that the Cuba of "love, peace, unity, [and] solidarity" had asserted itself.

———————

Due to its innovations in health care delivery, Cuba has been able to send its medical workers to other countries, including during the pandemic, to provide vital assistance. Cuba exports its medical workers, not terrorism. In the last days of the Trump administration, the U.S. government returned Cuba to its State Sponsors of Terrorism list. This was a vindictive act. Trump said it was because Cuba played host to guerrilla groups from Colombia, which was actually part of Cuba's role as host of the peace talks. Cuba played a key role in bringing peace in Colombia, a country that has been wracked by a terrible civil war since 1948 that claimed the lives of hundreds of thousands of people. The Biden administration continues to punish Cuba not for terrorism, but for the promotion of peace.

———————

The protests of July 2021 woke up the White House. Biden said that the protests were a "clarion call for freedom" and

White House officials said that Cuba was now a "top priority for the administration." But in what way was it a top priority? To use every means within the U.S. arsenal to overthrow the Cuban Revolution? Four new rounds of sanctions from July to August were placed on Cuban officials and Cuban institutions. And then, in February 2023, the United States renewed Cuba's place on the U.S. State Sponsors of Terrorism list.

Trump-Biden have pushed policies to starve Cuba of hard currency and to try to prevent the state from maintaining its commitment to education and health care, the pillars of the Cuban Revolution. Biden's "humanitarian parole program" allowed Cubans, Haitians, Nicaraguans, and Venezuelans to more easily migrate to the United States. The stated aim here is to attract teachers and medical personnel. Tougher sanctions, on top of the blockade, have made the fiscal position of the government very difficult, and with new incentives for migration it has challenged the Cuban Revolution at its core. This is Biden's goal, identical to U.S. policy since 1959.

Afterword

Cuba Is Not Alone

Occasionally, the people can break through. Cuba offers one of the most consistently poignant examples of this, which is precisely the source of its irritation to its much larger, capitalist neighbor. Cuba resisted assassinations and coups, blockades and sanctions. However flawed, it offered the world a vision of society beyond capitalist greed. It has produced a defiant society.

We should not exaggerate the isolation of the United States. It remains the country with the largest military force. It continues to dominate the channels for information. However, the U.S. wars in Iraq, Afghanistan, and Libya show us that the United States might be able to destroy countries, but it cannot rule them.

Where the United States *does* have an overwhelming advantage is in the battle of ideas. It is here that U.S. private companies dominate the hardware of communications (companies such as Facebook, Google, and Twitter as well as Zoom); it is here that U.S. media houses set the narrative for how to understand world events (houses such as CNN, the *New York Times*, Reuters, and the Associated Press). The process of manufacturing consent, which Noam first articulated many decades ago, still unfolds in the present.

The Cuban people face a great challenge in terms of how to put forward a view of their own process, their struggle to maintain the primacy of social life above money. Imperialism's "philosophy of dispossession," as Castro called it, is a philosophical attitude to the world that seeks to plunder both humanity and nature for private gain. A remarkable part of this story has been the resilience of the Cuban people—their ability to push back against the plunder. But it has to be acknowledged that the Cuban Revolution has been damaged by the wrath of the Godfather. Despite annual condemnation of the blockade by the world's nations, nothing seems to shift.

When I went to Cuba, I traveled around freely with a Canadian colleague who lived in Havana. We talked to people in different places. In health clinics we spoke to doctors, at a senior center we talked to retirees. We saw the modest gardens where people were growing food for their families. We went to the Martin Luther King Center to meet the people who work there to promote forms of social justice, including Reverend Raúl Suárez. I found Havana to be a well-ordered city, where people were carrying out their activities, and of course struggling under difficult circumstances. But we didn't see police standing around, didn't see the forces of repression everywhere. This was different from my experience in other places in the Third World such as Colombia and Haiti, or in refugee camps in Laos or Lebanon, where people feel like they are under bitter attack, barely surviving. I didn't sense that in Cuba. People seemed to be in tough circumstances, but nonetheless with light in their eyes, not fear and desolation. That's what is pretty amazing. You can't compare the attitude of people in Cuba and in Haiti. Cuba seemed hopeful; Haiti was in desolation.

Notes

Authors' Note: Our Essay on Cuba

1. William M. LeoGrande, *Our Own Backyard: The United States in Central America, 1977–1992* (Chapel Hill: University of North Carolina Press, 1998), 82.

2. Gardiner Harris, "16 Americans Sickened after Attack on Embassy Staff in Havana," *New York Times*, August 24, 2017; Julian E. Barnes and Adam Entous, "Foreign Adversaries 'Very Unlikely' to Blame for Havana Syndrome, Intelligence Review Finds," *New York Times*, March 1, 2023. See the Cuban Ministry of Foreign Affairs for the article, "Expertos señalan incongruencias en la hipótesis de los ataques acústicos," November 16, 2017.

3. Warren P. Strobel and Gordon Lubold, "Cuba to Host Secret Chinese Spy Base Focusing on US," *Wall Street Journal*, June 8, 2023, a story then amplified by the Editorial Board, "China's New Military Footprint in Cuba," *Wall Street Journal*, June 20, 2023.

4. "Residents of Bejucal, Cuba, Respond to US Allegations of Chinese Spy Base," BreakThrough News, June 16, 2023.

On Cuba

1. *The Kennedy Tapes: Inside the White House during the Cuban Missile Crisis*, ed. Ernest R. May and Philip D. Zelikow (Cambridge: Harvard University Press, 1997).

2. Andres Oppenheimer, *Castro's Final Hour* (New York: Simon and Schuster, 1992), 135.

3. John Quincy Adams, "Letter from John Quincy Adams, US Secretary of State, to Hugh Nelson, American Minister in Madrid, April 28, 1823," *Writings of John Quincy Adams*, volume 7, ed. Worthington Chauncey Ford (New York: Macmillan, 1917), 373.

4. Walter Johnson, *River of Dark Dreams: Slavery and Empire in the Cotton Kingdom* (Cambridge: Harvard University Press, 2013); Robert Mays, *Manifest Destiny's Underworld: Filibustering in Antebellum America* (Chapel Hill: University of North Carolina Press, 2002).

5. Allen Reed Millett, *The Politics of Intervention: The Military Occupation of Cuba, 1906–1909* (Columbus: Ohio State University Press, 1968).

6. Lars Schoultz, *The Infernal Little Cuban Republic: The United States and the Cuban Revolution* (Chapel Hill: University of North Carolina Press, 2009), 25.

7. Theodore Roosevelt, "1904: The Roosevelt Corollary to the Monroe Doctrine" in *Latin America and the United States: A Documentary History*, ed. Robert H. Holden and Eric Zolov (New York: Oxford University Press, 2000), 101.

8. Brian S. McBeth, *Dictatorship and Politics: Intrigue, Betrayal, and Survival in Venezuela, 1908–1935* (Notre Dame, IN: University of Notre Dame, 2008).

9. *The Presidential Recordings: John F. Kennedy, the Great Crises*, vol. 2, ed. Timothy Naftali and Philip Zelikow (New York: Norton, 2001), 416.

10. *The Presidential Recordings*, vol. 2, 442.

11. Enrique Circules, *The Mafia in Havana: A Caribbean Mob Story* (Melbourne: Ocean Press, 2003).

12. "Policy Recommendations for the Restoration of Normalcy in Cuba" (December 7, 1957), *Foreign Relations of the United States, 1955–1957, American Republics: Multilateral; Mexico; Caribbean,* vol. 6 (Washington, DC: U.S. Government Printing Office, 1987). Hereafter *FRUS.*

13. *The Kennedy Tapes,* 181.

14. Wayne Smith, *The Closest of Enemies: A Personal and Diplomatic Account of US-Cuban Relations Since 1957* (New York: Norton, 1987).

15. "Special National Intelligence Estimate" (March 22, 1960), *FRUS,* vol. 6, 870–71.

16. Stephen G. Rabe, "The Elusive Conference: United States Economic Relations with Latin America, 1945–1952," *Diplomatic History,* vol. 2, no. 3, summer 1978, 279–94.

17. Greg Grandin, *Empire's Workshop: Latin America, the United States, and the Rise of the New Imperialism* (New York: Holt Paperbacks, 2007).

18. All these documents are in William LeoGrande and Peter Kornbluh, *Back Channel to Cuba: The Hidden History of Negotiations between Washington and Havana* (Chapel Hill: University of North Carolina Press, 2015).

19. Harry Magdoff, *The Age of Imperialism: The Economics of U.S. Foreign Policy* (New York: Monthly Review Press, 1969).

20. Vijay Prashad, *Washington Bullets* (New Delhi: LeftWord Books, 2021).

21. J.P. Morrau, *The Second Revolution in Cuba* (New York: Monthly Review Press, 1962).

22. R. Hart Phillips, *Cuba, Island of Paradox* (New York: McDowell Oblensky, 1959), 335–36.

23. Gary DiGiuseppe, "Agribusiness: Why Cuba Should be Treated Like Other U.S. Trade Partners," *Arkansas Money and Politics*, June 1, 2016.

24. *Guatemala in Rebellion: Unfinished History*, ed. Jonathan L. Fried, Marvin E. Gettleman, Deborah Levenson-Estrada, and Nancy Peckenham (New York: Grove Press, 1983), 77–79.

25. Herbert Matthews, "Cuban Rebel Is Visited in Hideout. Castro Is Still Alive and Still Fighting in Mountains," *New York Times*, February 24, 1957, 1.

26. Fidel Castro, *La historia me absolvera* (La Habana: Impreso por Mendez y cia, n.d.), 13.

27. Paul Baran, *Reflections on the Cuban Revolution* (New York: Monthly Review Press, 1961); C. Wright Mills, *Listen Yankee: The Revolution in Cuba* (New York: McGraw Hill, 1960).

28. Claudio Pérez, "Apuntes de Ernesto Guevara: Guatemala (1953–1954) y la influencia en su trayectoria posterior," *X Jornadas de Sociología* (Buenos Aires: Facultad de Ciencias Sociales, Universidad de Buenos Aires, 2013).

29. Hugh Thomas, "Cuba, the United States and Batista, 1952–1958," *Cuban Communism, 1959–2003*, ed. Irving Louis Horowitz and Jaime Suchlicki (New Brunswick: Transaction, 2009), 16.

30. William Appleman Williams, *The United States, Cuba, and Castro: An Essay on the Dynamics of Revolution and the Dissolution of Empire* (New York: Monthly Review Press, 1962).

31. Ismael Zuaznábar, *La economía Cubana en la década del 50* (La Habana: Editorial de Ciencias Sociales, 1986).

32. Melchor W. Gastón, Oscar A. Echevarría, and René F. de la Huerta, *¿Por Qué Reforma Agraria?*, Serie-B, Apologética, folleto no. 23, (La Habana: Buró de Información y Propaganda, Agrupación Católica Universitaria, 1957), 6.

33. "Letter from the Ambassador in Cuba (Bonsal) to the Assistant Secretary of State for Inter-American Affairs (Rubottom)," Havana (August 2, 1960), *FRUS, 1958–1960, Cuba,* vol. 6 (1991).

34. "Despatch from the Embassy in Cuba to the Department of State, no. 1268," Havana (December 5, 1960), *FRUS,* vol. 6.

35. Jim Rasenberger, *The Brilliant Disaster: JFK, Castro, and America's Doomed Invasion of Cuba's Bay of Pigs* (New York: Scribner, 2012), 20.

36. Fabian Escalante, *Executive Action: 634 Ways to Kill Fidel Castro* (Melbourne: Ocean Press, 2006).

37. "Paper Prepared by the 5412 Committee. A Program of Covert Action Against the Castro Regime," Washington, DC (March 16, 1960), *FRUS, 1958–1960,* vol. 6.

38. Keith Bolender, *Stories from the Other Side: An Oral History of Terrorism Against Cuba* (London: Pluto Press, 2010).

39. Peter Kornbluh and Erin Maskell, *The CIA File on Luis Posada Carriles* (National Security Archive Electronic Briefing Book, no. 334, January 11, 2011); Peter Kornbluh, *Documents Linked*

to *Cuban Exile Luis Posada Highlighted Targets for Terrorism* (National Security Archive Briefing Book, no. 218, May 3, 2007).

40. "Letter dated 11 July 1960 from the Minister for Foreign Affairs of Cuba Addressed to the President of the Security Council," United Nations Security Council, s/4378, July 11, 1960.

41. "Memorandum of Discussion at the 451st Meeting of the National Security Council," Washington, DC (July 15, 1960), *FRUS, 1958–1960,* vol. 6.

42. Luke A. Nichter, *The Last Brahmin: Henry Cabot Lodge Jr. and the Making of the Cold War* (New Haven: Yale University Press, 2020).

43. "Paper Prepared by the 5412 Committee," March 16, 1960.

44. Stephen Kinzer and Stephen Schlesinger, *Bitter Fruit: The Story of the American Coup in Guatemala* (Cambridge: Harvard University Press, 2005).

45. Daniel Rubiera Zim, "Straining the Special Relationship: British and U.S. Policies Toward the Cuban Revolution, 1959–1961," *Cuban Studies*, vol. 33, 2002.

46. "Memorandum from the President's Special Assistant (Arthur Schlesinger) to President Kennedy," February 11, 1961, Kennedy Library, Arthur Schlesinger, Cuba 1961, Box 31, Top Secret.

47. Abraham Zaleznik, "The Education of Robert S. McNamara, Secretary of Defense, 1961–1968," *Revue française de gestion*, 159:6 (2005). Letters written by the Soviet ambassador to Cuba Sergey M. Kudryavtsev to Moscow reveal the closeness of the USSR to Cuba, but not that Cuba was "under the control" of the Soviets. McNamara repeated the basis for the U.S.-driven invasion of Cuba

in 1961 despite his own attempts in his memoir and interviews to distance himself from the "total failure."

48. "Memorandum," March 31, 1961, Box 300, Mansfield, Folder 536, Bowles Papers, Yale University.

49. Jonathan Nashel, *Edward Lansdale's Cold War* (Amherst: University of Massachusetts Press, 2005).

50. Jorge I. Domínguez, "The @#$%& Missile Crisis: Or, What Was 'Cuban' About U.S. Decisions During the Cuban Missile Crisis," *Diplomatic History*, vol. 24, no. 2, spring 2000, 312.

51. "Program Review by the Chief of Operations, Operation Mongoose (Lansdale)," Washington, DC (February 20, 1962), *FRUS, 1961–1963, vol. 10, Cuba, January 1961–September 1962.*

52. John Prados, *Safe for Democracy* (Lanham, MD: Rowman and Littlefield, 2006), 301.

53. "National Security Action Memorandum, no. 181," Washington, DC (August 23, 1962), *FRUS, 1961–1963, vol. 10, Cuba, January 1961–September 1962.*

54. Susan Williams, *White Malice: The CIA and the Covert Recolonization of Africa* (New York: Public Affairs, 2021).

55. Kudryavtsev's journal record of conversation with Roa, February 24, 1961, Arkhiv Vneshnei Politiki Rossiikoi Federatsii, F. 0104. Op. 17, P. 188, D. 3. II., 94–97.

56. Cody Fuelling, "To the Brink: Turkish and Cuban Missiles During the Height of the Cold War," *International Social Science Review*, 93:1 (2017).

57. Ruth Leacock, *Requiem for Revolution: The United States and Brazil, 1961–1969* (Kent, OH: Kent State University Press, 1990), 33.

58. "Transcript of a meeting at the White House, October 16, 1962," *FRUS, 1961–1963*, vol. 11, *Cuban Missile Crisis and Aftermath* (1996).

59. Raymond Garthoff, *Reflections on the Cuban Missile Crisis* (Washington, DC: Brookings Institution, 1989), 78–79.

60. Piero Gleijeses, *Conflicting Missions: Havana, Washington, and Africa, 1959–1976* (Chapel Hill: University of North Carolina Press, 2001), 26.

61. John Duncan Powell, "Militarism in Latin America," *Western Political Quarterly*, 18:2 (June 1965), 382–92.

62. Charles Maechling, "The Murderous Mind of the Latin Military," *Los Angeles Times*, March 18, 1982.

63. "The Coup Against the Third World: Chile, 1973," Dossier no. 68, Tricontinental: Institute for Social Research, September 2023.

64. Robert E. Looney, "The Role of Military Expenditures in Pre-Revolutionary Iran's Economic Decline," *Iranian Studies*, 21:3/4 (1988).

65. "Brazil Marks 50th Anniversary of Military Coup," ed. James G. Hershberg and Peter Kornbluh, National Security Archive Electronic Briefing Book, no. 465, April 2, 2014.

66. CLR James, *The Black Jacobins* (London: Vintage, 1963). Linking the Cuban Revolution into the Caribbean was also part of the framework of two important Caribbean political leaders, Juan Bosch from the Dominican Republic, who wrote *De Cris-*

tóbal Colón a Fidel Castro: el Caribe, frontera imperial (Madrid: Alfaguara, 1970), and Eric Williams from Trinidad and Tobago, who wrote *From Columbus to Castro: The History of the Caribbean, 1492–1969* (New York: Harper and Row, 1970).

67. Michel-Rolph Trouillot, *Haiti, Nation Against State: The Origins and Legacy of Duvalierism* (New York: Monthly Review Press, 1990), 102.

68. "Dispatch from the Ambassador in Haiti to the Department of State" (November 30, 1957), *FRUS, 1955–1957, American Republics: Multilateral; Mexico; Caribbean,* vol. 6 (1987).

69. Gérard Pierre-Charles, *Radiographie d'une dictature. Haïti et Duvalier* (Montreal: Les Editions Nouvelle Optique, 1973), 56.

70. Gérard Pierre-Charles, *Haïti Jamais Plus! Les Violations de droits de l'homme à l'époque des Duvaliers* (Port-au-Prince: Editions du Cresfed, 2000).

71. Josh Dewind and David Kinley, *Aiding Migration: The Impact of International Development Assistance on Haiti* (Boulder, CO: Westview Press, 1988), 61.

72. Americas Watch, *Haiti: Human Rights Under Hereditary Dictatorship* (New York: Americas Watch and the National Coalition for Haitian Refugees, 1985), 30.

73. Peter Hallward, *Damming the Flood: Haiti and the Politics of Containment* (London: Verso, 2007).

74. Sydney Freedberg and Rachel Swarns, "Poorly Enforced Sanctions Botch U.S. Embargo of Haiti," *Miami Herald,* November 3, 1994.

75. Catherine Porter, Constant Méheut, Matt Apuzzo, and Selam Gebrekidan, "The Root of Haiti's Misery: Reparations to Enslavers," *New York Times*, May 20, 2022.

76. Andres Schipani, "Haiti's economy held together by polo shirts and blue jeans," *Financial Times*, April 16, 2015.

77. Marylynn Steckley and Yasmine Shamsie, "Manufacturing Corporate Landscapes: The Case of Agrarian Displacement and Food (In)security in Haiti," *Third World Quarterly*, 36:1 (2015).

78. "Venezuela and Hybrid Wars in Latin America," Dossier no. 17, Tricontinental: Institute for Social Research, June 2019.

79. Prashad, *Washington Bullets*, 134–35.

80. James, *Black Jacobins*, 16.

81. Fidel Castro, *Palabras a los inteletuales* (La Habana: Ediciones Del Consejo Nacional De Cultura, 1961).

82. Dr. Siegfried Schnabl, *En defensa del amor* (La Habana: Editorial Científico-Técnica, 1981).

83. The *Washington Post* called the new Family Code "among the most progressive in Latin America." Mary Beth Sheridan, "Cuba Approves Same-Sex Marriage in Historic Turnabout," *Washington Post*, September 24, 2022.

84. "Record of Conversation between Mikoyan and Ernesto 'Che' Guevara, Havana, 16 November 1962," November 16, 1962, Wilson Center Digital Archive, from the personal papers of Dr. Sergo A. Mikoyan, donated to the National Security Archive, translation by Anna Melyakova for the National Security Archive. For an excellent overview of the debates in Cuba about development, see Helen Yaffe, *Che Guevara: The Economics of Revolution* (London: Palgrave, 2009).

85. Hugh Worrell Springer, *Reflections on the Failure of the First West Indian Federation* (New York: AMS, 1973).

86. Manuel Franco, et. al., "Impact of Energy Intake, Physical Activity, and Population-wide Weight Loss on Cardiovascular Disease and Diabetes Mortality in Cuba, 1980–2005," *American Journal of Epidemiology* 166:12 (December 2007); Manuel Franco, et. al., "Obesity Reduction and Its Possible Consequences: What Can We Learn from Cuba's Special Period?" *Canadian Medical Association Journal*, 178:8 (April 2008).

87. Richard Levins, *Talking About Trees: Science, Ecology, and Agriculture in Cuba* (Delhi: LeftWord Books, 2008).

88. Polly Pattullo, *Last Resorts: The Cost of Tourism in the Caribbean* (Jamaica: Ian Randle, 1996).

89. "Cuba. Helms Threatens Castro," *Time*, February 9, 1995.

90. Jurek Martin and Nancy Dunne, "Clinton Postpones Court Action over U.S. AntiCuba Law," *Financial Times*, July 17, 1996.

91. "President's Statement on Helms-Burton Suspension," January 3, 1997.

92. David Fox, "European Commission Welcomes Cuba Law Suspension," Reuters, January 3, 1997.

93. Letter to President Clinton from the National Foreign Trade Council, Organization for International Investment, U.S. Chamber of Commerce, European American Chamber of Commerce, and U.S. Council for International Business, July 1, 1996.

94. Frank Prial, "UN Votes to Urge US to Dismantle Embargo on Cuba," *New York Times*, November 25, 1992.

95. Julio García Espinoza, "Por Un Cine Imperfecto" (1969), *Hojas de Cine. Testimonios y documentos del nuevo cine latinoamericano* (México: Unam, 1988), 63–79.

96. The material in this section is from Piero Gleijeses, *Visions of Freedom: Havana, Washington, Pretoria, and the Struggle for South Africa, 1976–1991* (Chapel Hill: University of North Carolina Press, 2013).

97. Fidel Castro with Ignacio Ramonet, *My Life. A Spoken Autobiography* (New York: Scribner, 2006), 326–34.

98. Isaac Saney, *Cuba, Africa, and Apartheid's End: Africa's Children Return!* (Lanham, MD: Lexington Books, 2023), 4–5.

99. E.J. Dionne, "Inevitably, the Politics of Terror: Fear Has Become Part of Washington's Power Struggle," Brookings Institution, May 25, 2003.

100. Anthony Lake, "Confronting Backlash States," *Foreign Affairs*, March/April 1994.

101. "4 Treasury Agents Track Saddam, bin Laden Funds; 21 Work Castro," *Associated Press*, April 30, 2004.

102. "Senators Reject Administration's 'Cuba Commission' Recommendations," U.S. Senate Committee on Finance, May 6, 2004.

103. Pamela Falk, "Eyes on Cuba: U.S. Business and the Embargo," *Foreign Affairs*, 75:2 (1996); Carl Nagin, "Annals of Diplomacy," *New Yorker*, January 26, 1998.

104. Jeff Mason and David Alexander, "Obama Seeks 'New Beginning' with Cuba," Reuters, April 17, 2009.

105. Mark Felsenthal, "Obama Says U.S. Needs to Update Policies on Cuba," Reuters, November 9, 2013.

106. "Statement by the President on Cuba Policy Changes," White House, December 17, 2014.

107. Mauricio Claver-Carone, "Obama's Cuba Policy Makes a Bad Situation Worse," *Miami Herald*, November 16, 2016.

108. "National Security Presidential Memorandum on Strengthening the Policy of the United States Toward Cuba," White House, June 16, 2017.

109. Emilio Morales, "Remittances: An Investment Route for Cubans?," Havana Consulting Group, September 27, 2019.

110. Mariakarla Nodarse Venancio and Alex Bare, "The Human Cost of Cuba's Inclusion on the State Sponsors of Terrorism List," Washington Office of Latin America, March 28, 2023.

About the Authors

Noam Chomsky is Institute Professor (emeritus) in the Department of Linguistics and Philosophy at the Massachusetts Institute of Technology and Laureate Professor of Linguistics and Agnese Nelms Haury Chair in the Program in Environment and Social Justice at the University of Arizona. A world-renowned linguist and political activist, he is the author of numerous books, including *On Language, Understanding Power* (edited by Peter R. Mitchell and John Schoeffel), *American Power and the New Mandarins, For Reasons of State, Problems of Knowledge and Freedom, Objectivity and Liberal Scholarship, Towards a New Cold War, The Essential Chomsky* (edited by Anthony Arnove), *On Anarchism, The Chomsky-Foucault Debate* (with Michel Foucault), and *The Withdrawal: Iraq, Libya, Afghanistan, and the Fragility of U.S. Power* (with Vijay Prashad). He lives in Tucson, Arizona.

Vijay Prashad is director of Tricontinental: Institute for Social Research, editor of LeftWord Books, and chief correspondent for Globetrotter. He is the author of *Uncle Swami: South Asians in America Today*, *The Darker Nations: A People's History of the Third World* (winner of the Muzaffar Ahmad Book Prize), *The Karma of Brown Folk*, and *The Withdrawal: Iraq, Libya, Afghanistan, and the Fragility of U.S. Power* (with Noam Chomsky). He lives in Santiago, Chile.

Publishing in the Public Interest

Thank you for reading this book published by The New Press. The New Press is a nonprofit, public interest publisher. New Press books and authors play a crucial role in sparking conversations about the key political and social issues of our day.

We hope you enjoyed this book and that you will stay in touch with The New Press. Here are a few ways to stay up to date with our books, events, and the issues we cover:

- Sign up at www.thenewpress.com/subscribe to receive updates on New Press authors and issues and to be notified about local events
- Like us on Facebook: www.facebook.com/newpress-books
- Follow us on Twitter: www.twitter.com/thenewpress
- Follow us on Instagram: www.instagram.com/thenew-press

Please consider buying New Press books for yourself; for friends and family; or to donate to schools, libraries, community centers, prison libraries, and other organizations involved with the issues our authors write about.

The New Press is a 501(c)(3) nonprofit organization. You can also support our work with a tax-deductible gift by visiting www.thenewpress.com/donate.